SHAKESPEARE

THE LANDMARK LIBRARY

Chapters in the History of Civilization

The Landmark Library is a record of the achievements of humankind from the late Stone Age to the present day. Each volume in the series is devoted to a crucial theme in the history of civilization, and offers a concise and authoritative text accompanied by a generous complement of images. Contributing authors to The Landmark Library are chosen for their ability to combine scholarship with a flair for communicating their specialist knowledge to a wider, non-specialist readership.

SHAKESPEARE

The Theatre of Our World

PETER CONRAD

HEAD
of ZEUS

An Apollo Book

To the Reader.

This Figure, that thou here seest put
      It was for gentle Shakespeare cu
Wherein the Grauer had a strife
      with Nature, to out-doo the life
O, could he but haue drawne his wit
      As well in brasse, as he hath hit
His face; the Print would then surpa
      All, that was euer writ in brasse.
But, since he cannot, Reader, looke
      Not on his Picture, but his Book.

B. I

Mr. WILLIAM
SHAKESPEARES

COMEDIES,
HISTORIES, &
TRAGEDIES.

Published according to the True Originall Copies.

Martin Droeshout sculpsit London.

LONDON
Printed by Isaac Iaggard, and Ed. Blount. 1623.

PREVIOUS PAGES
The First Folio.

IMAGE CREDITS
p. 13 Colin Underhill/Alamy Stock Photo; p. 14
Corbis/Getty Images; pp. 18–19 Art Collection/
Alamy Stock Photo; p. 21 British Museum;
p. 22 Topfoto.co.uk; p. 24 Topfoto.co.uk;
p. 28 © Shakespeare Birthplace Trust; p. 35
Shutterstock; p. 38 © Victoria and Albert
Museum, London; pp. 46–7 Shutterstock;
p. 99 Angus McBean © RSC; pp. 116–17
Shutterstock; p. 143 Alamy Stock Photo; p. 162
Getty Images; pp. 176–7 Colección de Arte
Amalia Lacroze de Fortabat; pp. 178–9 © Tate
Britain; pp. 182–3 © Tate Britain; pp. 186–7 ©
Tate Britain; p. 192 © The Makins Collection/
Bridgeman Images; p. 195 © 2018. The
Metropolitan Museum of Art/Art Resource/
Scala, Florence; pp. 202–3 Getty Images; pp.
210–11 Alamy Stock Photo; pp. 220–1 Alamy
Stock Photo; pp. 226–7 Topfoto.co.uk; pp.
236–7 Shutterstock; pp. 242–3 Reg Wilson ©
RSC; pp. 246–7 Sara Krulwich/New York
Times.

So Long Lives This

Shakespeare forever
Unlikely likenesses
Author and actor
The poet-priest
Disbelievers

At the National Theatre in London, a stone plaque in the foyer dedicates – no, consecrates – the building 'TO THE LIVING MEMORY OF WILLIAM SHAKESPEARE'. The solemn phrase conjures up a spirit, as if calling on Shakespeare to patrol the theatre's angular concrete ramparts, like the ghost at Elsinore who asks to be remembered before disappearing. A mile away, Shakespeare is a less spectral presence at his own reconstructed Globe, where his name and his lean, goateed face sell branded merchandise that includes chocolate bars, sweatshirts, beanies, cufflinks, earrings, coffee mugs, fridge magnets, plastic bath ducks, and skeletal ceramic heads with slots in the rear for use as money boxes.

Shakespeare might have been surprised to find himself so piously and profitably commemorated. One of his sonnets predicts that 'So long as men can breathe, or eyes can see, / So long lives this', but his plays are haunted and yet acerbically amused by temporariness: in the scene that almost allegorically sums up Shakespearean drama, a man holds a skull in his hand and tells it jokes. Metaphors abrade and corrode the language Shakespeare's characters use. The Duke in *Measure for Measure* assures Angelo that his name will be eternalized in 'characters of brass', securing for him

> A forted residence 'gainst the tooth of time
> And razure of oblivion.

But burnished metal and castellated architecture are no defence: time gnaws at us, or erases us with a cruel, razory implement. Love, belying the sonnet's assurance, cannot resist this unsparing force. At the beginning of *All's Well That Ends Well*, Helena, having mourned her adored father for six months, asks herself 'What was he like?' With a shamed candour that instantly establishes her raw human truth, she admits 'I have forgot him.'

When Shakespeare died in 1616, he was probably resigned to the same fate. Unlike Ben Jonson, he did not safeguard his work by collecting his plays in print; it was the actors John Heminges and Henry Condell who assembled the First Folio in 1623, and we have them to thank for preserving literature's most dramatically vital and poetically intricate account of our human world. Four centuries later, Shakespeare himself is reverently remembered, but his characters are still alive, thriving inside us. Macbeth says that his imaginary dagger 'marshall'st me the way that I was going', and for good or ill the people in the plays perform the same service. From Romeo we learn about a man's emotional awakening, while Hamlet exposes our internal conflicts and Richard III shows us, if we are that way inclined, how to convert debilities and disadvantages into sources of power. Cordelia and her sisters suggest a range of responses to a social order invidiously ruled by fathers. Cleopatra and Lady Macbeth – a voluptuous goddess and a killer who despises 'the milk of human kindness' – are outlying female archetypes. Rosalind with her manifold affections and her generous adaptability is an Everywoman or perhaps, because of her androgyny, an Everyperson. Falstaff smiles at the world, Lear berates it, and Feste in his parting song at the end of *Twelfth Night* jauntily copes with its sodden daily disappointments. These imaginary beings, taking on flesh in the theatre, have shaped our understanding of love and death or consciousness and morality; they demonstrate how singular we are, and also what a plurality of selves we possess.

The Shakespearean stage is a playground for alternate identities, and as his actors experimentally reveal or conceal themselves and assume or swap roles, we come to see that our existence is a dramatic exercise, requiring us, as Bottom says, to 'rehearse most obscenely and courageously'. Prospero writes the script and engages others 'to enact / My present fancies'; Puck chaotically directs the show; Iago, 'nothing if not critical', scribbles notes as he watches from the sidelines. We can choose who to be, but during a lifelong performance we are likely to adopt all those parts, successively or simultaneously. Whatever we experience will have been anticipated by a character in one of the plays, and expressed with such force or pathos or witty brevity that, when the occasion arises, we only need the living memory of a quotation. It sometimes seems as if Shakespeare created us all.

*

Heminges and Condell compiled the Folio to honour 'the memory of so worthy a friend and fellow', yet they left Shakespeare indistinct. What, to ask Helena's question, was he like?

We know little enough about him; ultimately he may be unknowable. His origins were ordinary, his life professionally busy but otherwise uneventful. He was neither glamorous like the universally admired Philip Sidney, nor scandalous like Christopher Marlowe with his provocative opinions and his violent end in a tavern brawl. The traces Shakespeare left are mostly financial: records of taxes owed or properties purchased, a will that is seemingly ungenerous to his wife Anne Hathaway. Some spurious anecdotes enliven the annals. Gossip alleges that he stole a deer in Stratford-upon-Avon in his youth and later shared a mistress in London with Richard Burbage, the actor who played many of his tragic roles. His testimony in a legal case that involved his landlady's daughter was terse, and in one instance the clerk noted that he 'remembereth not'. When he signed the transcript, he abbreviated his name to 'Wllm Shakp' – negligent haste, or a ghostly vanishing act?

William Hazlitt, the most psychologically acute of Shakespeare's nineteenth-century critics, rightly celebrated the idiosyncrasy of his characters – Hamlet with his whimsies, Cleopatra with her wiles, the volcanic pique of Coriolanus – and said that

Gheeraert Janssen's monument in Holy Trinity Church,
Stratford-upon-Avon.

IVDICIO PYLIVM GENIO SOCRATEM, ARTE MARONEM,
TERRA TEGIT, POPVLVS MÆRET, OLYMPVS HABET

STAY PASSENGER, WHY GOEST THOV BY SO FAST,
READ IF THOV CANST, WHOM ENVIOVS DEATH HATH PLAST
WITH IN THIS MONVMENT SHAKSPEARE: WITH WHOME,
QVICK NATVRE DIDE WHOSE, NAME, DOTH DECK Ý TOMBE,
FAR MORE, THEN COST: SIEH ALL, Ý HE HATH WRITT,
LEAVES LIVING ART, BVT PAGE, TO SERVE HIS WITT.

OBIT AÑO DO 1616
ÆTATIS 53 DIE 23 AP.

The Cloud capt Towers
The Gorgeous Palaces
The Solemn Temples,
The Great Globe itself,
Yea all which it Inherit
Shall Dissolve
And like the baseless fabrick of a Vision
Leave not a wreck behind

GVL: KENT INV:

P. SCHEEMAKERS
MDCCXL

each of them was 'absolutely independent of the rest, as well as of the author', who did not share their outsized eccentricity. Shakespeare, Hazlitt suggested, must have been 'just like any other man', with the proviso that 'he was like all other men' – an impossible compendium of the divergent, incompatible people in his plays. The man with a thousand faces is effectively faceless, so Hazlitt proposed that we should think of Shakespeare abstractly, picturing him as 'the tallest, the strongest, the most graceful and beautiful' of 'a race of giants'.

Early portraits, however, were stubbornly uncharismatic. Martin Droeshout's engraving in the Folio gives Shakespeare leaden eyes in a thin, unamused face, with hair as stiff as a bad wig; his ruff threatens to slice off his head. Chubbier and ruddier, the bust by Gheeraert Janssen in the church at Stratford presents him as a provincial worthy, holding a quill that seems ready to tabulate accounts or take minutes at a committee meeting. What we cannot see is the mind behind the facial mask. Victor Hugo, who in his worshipful fervour described the plays as an 'indirect divine creation', compared Shakespeare's brain to a virgin forest and a turbulent ocean, or described him as a condor swooping and soaring. The man portrayed by Droeshout and Janssen looks less elemental and aquiline.

For his contemporaries, Shakespeare was not superhuman, and his canonization happened gradually and a little grudgingly. Ben Jonson regretted his death, but noted that Chaucer and Spenser had not been edged aside to make room for him in Westminster Abbey, so he remained 'a monument without a tomb'; Milton defensively argued that Shakespeare needed no 'star-ypointing pyramid'. Did he even deserve one? The literary corner in Westminster Abbey was reserved for poets, whose art had a classical pedigree, and who, like Milton, regarded the quest for fame as a noble motive. Dramatists practised a newer and more ignoble trade, hustled by commerce and the demands of

Peter Scheemakers's monument in Westminster Abbey.

customers, which made plays as disposable as popular songs or other seasonal offerings.

Nevertheless, by the mid-eighteenth century Shakespeare had begun – as Samuel Johnson observed, not without surprise – to 'assume the dignity of an ancient', which entitled him to 'the privilege of… prescriptive veneration'. Monuments were called for, and memorialists had to decide how an eternalized Shakespeare ought to look. A statue was at last installed in Westminster Abbey in 1741. Sculpted by Peter Scheemakers, Shakespeare here bends sideways under the weight of posterity's expectations, leaning on a pile of the collected works that he never saw in print. A dagger, the emblem of tragedy, grazes a laurel wreath that he is not wearing: has he declined the exalted status wished on him? He points to an unfurling scroll that for a long while remained blank, since there was no consensus about what Shakespeare's testamentary statement should be. Eventually Prospero's preview of universal dissolution in *The Tempest* was painted onto the marble page. The nihilism of this speech, which curtails a magic show, comes as a shock: is human life really an 'insubstantial pageant', as transitory as the performance of a play? And doesn't that ghoulishly subvert the only too substantial pageants staged in the abbey on state occasions? Aptly enough, fulfilling Prospero's prophecy about 'the baseless fabric' of his vision, the lettering has partly rubbed off the scroll.

In 1836 Samuel Colman painted a sublime apocalypse entitled *The Edge of Doom*, taking his title from a sonnet in which Shakespeare swears that love will persist 'even to the edge of doom'. Uninterested in love but excited by doom, Colman imagined mountains collapsing as the sky falls in on a city scorched by lightning bolts. The poem refers to the slow, erosive power of time's sickle; the painting more impatiently brings the world to a sudden, blazing end. Among toppled carriages and shattered columns, one object is still intact: Scheemakers'

Shakespeare from Westminster Abbey. Despite the conflagration, the marble figure maintains its poise – an ultimate memento of perishable civilization, even though all copies of Shakespeare plays have presumably been incinerated in the city's burning libraries.

Statues mortify the human beings whose flesh they turn to stone, weighing them down with a symbolic burden. Louis-François Roubiliac's Shakespeare, now in the British Library, is at least permitted to relax, rather than being forced to plead mankind's case on the day of judgement. The posture of Roubiliac's figure is willowy, with one of his slippers half off; pretending to write, he uses his spare hand as a pensive support for his chin. He attitudinizes for the sculptor's benefit, though this preening self-awareness was wished on Shakespeare by the actor David Garrick, who commissioned Roubiliac in 1758 and volunteered as his model. A more self-absorbed Shakespeare, sculpted by John Quincy Adams Ward, was set up in New York in 1872. Out for a stroll on the Literary Mall in Central Park, Ward's figure has one hand earnestly placed on his heart, while the other holds a book. He might be mimicking Hamlet, who promenades while reading to convince Polonius of his distracted melancholia. Ronald Gower's Shakespeare, placed in a Stratford garden in 1887, is not a reader but an omnific creator. Veneration has led to levitation: seated on a pedestal, Shakespeare here surveys four characters who occupy lower plinths of their own at the end of radial paths. Arranged in a global circle, they mark the outer limits of his intellectual world. Hamlet brooding over Yorick's skull represents Philosophy, and vigorous Prince Hal is History; gripping her wrist because she cannot wash her bronze hands, Lady Macbeth stands for Tragedy, while big-bellied Falstaff embodies Comedy.

At Southwark Cathedral, Henry McCarthy's monument, completed in 1912, eases Shakespeare into eternity by making him lie down in a coffin-shaped recess. But he is not yet ready for the

overleaf
Shakespeare on Doomsday, painted by Samuel Colman.

mausoleum: he props himself on an elbow, and in his open hand he sometimes holds a sprig of fresh rosemary, a token of remembrance donated by a devotee. Earlier, a Victorian stained-glass window directly above gave Shakespeare a celestial patron: he stood beside an enthroned Muse of Poetry with a dove above her head, which made him a conduit for doctrinal verities. In 1954, when the window was replaced, Christopher Webb's new design left out this literary version of the Holy Spirit, although Webb's Prospero resembles a priest raising his arms in prayer, while Ariel in a streak of light might be mistaken for the Pentecostal dove. But the cathedral no longer equates art with Gospel truth, and infidels are not debarred. Webb's modern congregation includes a simian Caliban, a wracked, pallid Lady Macbeth, and Falstaff filling out an infernally vivid scarlet tunic. Only the author is absent from the window, and his multifarious characters – who preen in cross garters or bemoan a lost warhorse, caper in a jester's costume or come to terms with a suddenly furry head and lengthened, flapping ears – are too intent on their own affairs to bother searching for him.

*

If Shakespeare eludes us, it is because he was evasive on purpose. Wordsworth, for whom poetry consisted of lyrical confession, believed that in the sonnets 'Shakespeare unlocked his heart'; Robert Browning countered by saying 'If so, the less Shakespeare he!'

A typical sonnet by Shakespeare begins with a gesture that feels impulsive and self-revealing – 'Farewell! thou art too dear for my possessing', or 'Alas, 'tis true, I have gone here and there / And made myself a motley to the view', which seems to lament a life of self-squandering on stage. But as the regularity of the poetic form takes over, an emotion that initially sounds private or

Louis-François Roubiliac's monument.

intimate is analytically dissected or rhetorically teased out through three quatrains until in a final couplet it becomes impersonal, applicable to whoever chooses to share it:

> For as the sun is daily new and old,
> So is my love still telling what is told.

Sometimes the conclusion is proverbial, a domestic commonplace rather than the product of some secret crisis. The ninety-fifth sonnet starts with a lacerating attack on sexual treachery, but ends by warning that 'The hardest knife ill used doth lose his edge', which is true in the kitchen and perhaps also in bed. The I has become an other, anybody or nobody.

The Prologue in *Troilus and Cressida* appears dressed in armour, and explains that this is not 'in confidence of author's pen or actor's voice'. Text and performance are managed by two different beings, separate aspects of a co-operative creation; the Prologue is embarrassed to be in limbo, neither the writer of the speech he delivers nor a participant in the play. Despite this shiftiness, the distinction is crucial for Shakespeare, even when he writes a poem in the first person. Author hides behind actor, the pen silently inscribes lines to be spoken by an alter ego. Illicit glimpses of the dramatist's emotional life should not be expected.

Thomas Carlyle thought that Shakespeare must have possessed a 'joyful tranquillity', so 'quiet, complete and self-sufficing' that he might never have written a word if he had not been prosecuted for deer-poaching, which forced him to make a living outside Stratford. This fanciful scenario flirts with primal mysteries. Why, after all, should God – also presumably self-sufficient and joyfully tranquil before making the world – have bothered to create the vexatious human race? Uncertainty or lack of information has licensed delusional theories that Shakespeare's plays were written by someone with a better education and

The memorial window at Southwark Cathedral, with Henry McCarthy's monument glossier social connections, such as Marlowe, Francis Bacon, or the courtier Edward de Vere. Henry James could not reconcile 'the divine William' with 'the man from Stratford', and suspected that Shakespeare might be 'the biggest and most successful fraud ever practised on a patient world'.

The Victorian painter Ford Madox Brown was troubled by 'the want of a credible likeness of our national poet': the want of credibility was a temptation to disbelief or outright atheism, and could not be tolerated. Scheemakers' pensive sage and Roubiliac's dapper wit hardly qualified as credible likenesses, so in 1849 Brown made good the deficiency by producing an imaginary portrait of Shakespeare. He merged features from Droeshout's bony engraving and Janssen's better-fed bust, and hired a professional model to give bullish solidity to the identikit image. The figure's right hand rests on a desk near a row of the books Shakespeare used as sources – Plutarch's lives of the Greeks and Romans, collected tales by Chaucer and Boccaccio, the essays by Montaigne that Hamlet must have read – though this makes him look like a doughty Shakespearean scholar in doctoral robes. Behind the desk, a trumpeter on a tapestry blows a fanfare, synonymous with fame and honour, and holds up a laurel wreath for the ceremonial coronation. An investiture is taking place, and the stern, forthright stare of the laureate dares us to doubt him – but the twirly upturned ends of his moustache hint at a suppressed smile, signalling that he is an imposter, like Garrick dressing up for Roubiliac. Shakespeare was an actor, a professional dissimulator; the self may have been just another role to be played or a mask to be worn.

In Virginia Woolf's novel *Orlando* an anonymous figure is spotted in the servants' hall of a stately home. By contrast with Ford Madox Brown's grandee, he is 'rather fat, shabby', wears a dirty ruff, and has a tankard beside him as he fiddles with his pen. His eyes are said to be 'globed', which offers a clue to his identity.

Shakespeare as imagined by Ford Madox Brown in 1849.

Unimpressed, not recognizing the man whom he later ranks among 'his favourite heroes', Orlando turns away. That abortive encounter is a caution for Shakespeare's biographers: how can they not be baffled by a subject so impenetrable and outwardly unremarkable? Ernest Dowden, in a study published in 1875, tried to solve the problem by treating Shakespeare's life as an allegorical progress through the ages of man. The plays, in this reading, follow him from juvenile comic optimism to the middle-aged crises of tragedy, before he attains the beatific elderly serenity that Dowden took to be the mood of *The Tempest*. True, each of us performs several parts in the course of our lives, adopting the appropriate roles in an orderly succession as the decades pass, but Dowden's assumption slights Shakespeare's dramatic imagination, or else condemns him to reel through all the ecstasies and agonies that he assigns to his characters. Dickens felt possessed by a demon while writing about the malevolent dwarf Quilp in *The Old Curiosity Shop*, and later wrecked his health with his overwrought public performances of Nancy's murder by Sikes in *Oliver Twist*. Shakespeare gave birth to freaks, imps and monsters with no apparent loss of mental equanimity.

Although Ben Jonson admired Shakespeare, he insisted on remaining 'this side Idolatry'. Bardolatry, as George Bernard Shaw came to call it, soon overleapt that measured tribute. In 1664 John Dryden declared that Shakespeare possessed 'a larger soul of poesy than any ever of our nation'. Garrick scanned a remoter past when he asserted that Shakespeare was 'the first Genius since the Creation': God created the earth, and at length the dramatist peopled it. In 1769 in Stratford, at a belated celebration of Shakespeare's Jubilee, Garrick recited a *Dedication Ode* that excitedly greeted the 'blest genius of the isle'. ''Tis he! 'Tis he!' Garrick cried, like Hamlet identifying his father's ghost. The necromantic summons reached its climax when Garrick triply intoned that 'lov'd, rever'd, immortal name' – 'SHAKESPEARE!

SHAKESPEARE! SHAKESPEARE!' – as drums and trumpets solemnized the invocation. Emulating Garrick's tribute, in 1771 Goethe delivered an oration that hailed Shakespeare as a creator from Hellenic not Hebraic myth. Like Prometheus, Goethe said, Shakespeare murkily shaped clay into human form, then breathed life and language into his colossi. Thomas Linley's *Lyric Ode*, performed at Drury Lane in 1776, presented Shakespeare's nativity as a rehearsal for Christ's second coming. 'Be Shakespeare born!' commands Linley's chorus, and God's 'fav'rite son', humanity's anointed apologist, descends to earth in Stratford not Bethlehem. Appropriately enough, the celebration of Shakespeare's tercentenary at Stratford in 1864 culminated in a performance of Handel's *Messiah*. No play could have provided the requisite uplift: Feste's disconsolate song about the rain that has been falling since the world began is hardly a 'Hallelujah', and Prospero's morose farewell leads to no 'Amen'.

As the Old Testament deity lost credence in the later nineteenth century, a new king of glory filled the gap. For Carlyle, Shakespeare had taken holy orders as the 'melodious Priest of a *true* Catholicism'; his 'universal Psalm' was more ecumenical than scripture, and by comparison the Koran seemed to Carlyle 'a stupid piece of prolix absurdity'. Hubert Parry set four of Shakespeare's sonnets to music in 1887, treating them as sermons on loss and consolation, addressed less to a distant beloved than to a retreating God. Those who wanted to believe in a creator believed in Shakespeare – on his deathbed in 1892, Tennyson is said to have cried out 'Where is Shakespeare? I must have my Shakespeare!' – and those who renounced religious belief also stopped believing in him. After developing his theory of evolution, Darwin abandoned his earlier love of Shakespeare, by whom he confessed he was now bored or even 'nauseated'. Since there was no divine maker, how could he honour this bounteous literary begetter?

A sonnet by Matthew Arnold made amends for God's demise by endowing Shakespeare with the enigmatic serenity of a Buddha. He responds to our questions with a mute smile, but

> All pains the immortal spirit must endure,
> All weakness which impairs, all griefs which bow,
> Find their sole speech in that victorious brow.

Arnold prefers the 'sole speech' of that silent, statuesque face to the eloquence of the characters in the plays; ignoring the comedies, he emphasizes Shakespeare's tragic ministry to our godless world, where he watches over 'the foil'd searching of mortality'.

The most dedicated mortal searchers were already travelling as pilgrims to Shakespeare's birthplace in a Midlands town that he must have been eager to leave: Stratford, in a phrase of Henry James's, had become 'the Mecca of the English-speaking race'. Tourists to this ersatz holy city climbed stairs to look around empty rooms in reconstructed houses that Shakespeare had once occupied, and meditated at his tomb in the church, as Walter Scott is seen doing in a painting attributed to David Roberts. A trip to the theatre was no part of the itinerary: the seekers paid homage to the mystique of a hidden god, rather than sampling Shakespeare's irrepressibly lively representation of our human world.

*

A few heretics challenged what Carlyle called the 'state Hero-worship' of Shakespeare. They understandably resisted an orthodoxy that can be automatic and unfelt; their arguments have value because they force us to redefine why Shakespeare matters.

In old age Tolstoy railed at him as 'a bad writer'. Lear's ravings disgusted Tolstoy, and he could only tolerate the jokes and puns in the plays when they were voiced by the sleazy toper Falstaff.

Walter Scott paying homage in the church at Stratford.

Hamlet, he thought, had 'no character'– but don't we all, like the self-contradictory prince, contain a set of uncoordinated selves? As a Christian convert, Tolstoy abhorred Shakespeare's lack of 'ethical authority' and 'religious consciousness'. His complaint missed the point of Shakespearean drama, which supplanted the cycles of medieval plays that expounded scriptural parables. Fables about a generic Everyman – whose arraignment by God is acted out in the early-sixteenth-century morality play – were replaced by accounts of individual men and women, often amoral and almost always irreligious.

Shaw commended the author of *Everyman*, whoever he might have been, as 'an artist-philosopher', which Shakespeare was not. In Shaw's opinion, Shakespeare viewed the world as a 'stage of fools' because he could find no purpose in our earthly farrago of misery and mirth, and 'could see no sense in living'. All it takes to refute this is to remember the happiness of Viola and Sebastian when they are reunited in *Twelfth Night*, or of Leontes when Hermione is miraculously restored to him in *The Winter's Tale*. Hymen in *As You Like It* says that there is 'mirth in heaven / When earthly things, made even, / Atone together', and sometimes that divine comedy is re-enacted here below.

More plausibly, Shaw objected that Shakespeare was 'concerned with the diversities of the world instead of with its unities'. That at least is true, and not necessarily a demerit. Shakespeare ignored the unities of time and place that classical plays were obliged to respect, and loosened form to show that life is contradictory, uncontainable, regulated by no God and not directed either, as Shaw wished, by a sense of mission. Shaw's own characters are unitarians, fiercely single-minded like Saint Joan; Shakespeare's characters are diversifiers. Hamlet, with a job of revenge to do, can't help being distracted by amusing detours, just as Lear in his madness keeps remembering things he has taken 'too little care of' – naked wretches who need to be housed, a mouse that might appreciate a piece of toasted cheese. Why has Helena forgotten her father? Because her head is now full of the obnoxious but attractive Bertram. Human beings, as Falstaff says, are 'foolish-compounded clay', tragic at times of crisis but mostly comic when responding to upsets and embarrassments. The choice between Shakespeare and Shaw depends on how you view life, and also on what you expect from literature – sympathy or stringency, an open-armed acceptance of imperfection or an insistence that we should always strive, like Nietzsche's supermen, to reach dizzier mental altitudes.

Irreverent rather than outraged like Tolstoy, Shaw accused Shakespeare of typically English vices: snobbery, mercantile moralism, a bluff dislike of intellect. He saw the plays as an arena for 'instinctive temperaments' – the ruffian Coriolanus, Bottom the roisterer – not a forum for argument. A competitive impudence underlay these cheeky criticisms. 'Better than Shakespeare?' asked Shaw in one of his prefaces; he answered the question not, like the neoclassicists, by rewriting the plays but by reforming their wayward protagonists. *Caesar and Cleopatra* excludes Antony and his gaudy nights with Cleopatra; instead Shaw studies the chaste relationship between the philosophical conqueror and a kittenish young queen who under his influence turns 'prosy and serious and learned'. In *Heartbreak House*, Lear outgrows his futile tantrums and waits for the world to end in a bomb blast, not a storm. The unequal combat concludes in *Shakes versus Shav*, a skit for belligerent puppets written by Shaw in 1949. Shakes goads Shav to fight, then complains because his opponent, being three centuries younger, can punch harder. Shav jeers that his rival, 'dead and turned to clay, / May stop a hole to keep the wind away'. Shakes points out that he said so first, then quotes himself again – 'Out, out, brief candle!' – to plunge them both into darkness. Shaw refused to think of life as a flickering candle flame. He considered our existence 'a splendid torch' that he brandished in a relay race, but he had the good sense to allow Shakespeare the last word.

Bertolt Brecht's misgivings were political. He worried about Shakespeare's concentration on great or grandiose individuals – royal dilettantes like the 'introspective sponger' Hamlet, or ruffians like Macbeth – and said that our enjoyment of their downfall produced a pointlessly negative 'drama for cannibals'. These socialist scruples did not reckon with the all-inclusive sympathy of the plays. Brutus in *Julius Caesar* feels ashamed of over-taxing his young attendant Lucius, and in *King Lear* servants triage the blinded Gloucester with flax and whites of eggs. Even the soldier who is ordered to hang Cordelia calls it 'man's work', unlike the agricultural drudgery from which he has escaped, and gives that as his reason for obeying; killed by Lear, he becomes one of the tragedy's collateral victims.

D. H. Lawrence complained in a versified squib 'How boring, how small Shakespeare's people are!', even though they 'muse and thunder / In such lovely language'. Yet their humbling physical defects humanize them: Julius Caesar's deaf ear, Gloucester's aged and 'corky' arms, the supposed toothache that keeps Iago awake when he lodges with Cassio, the catarrh that makes Othello ask for Desdemona's handkerchief, even Hamlet's corpulence, about which his mother indulgently jokes during the fencing match. Triviality endears them to us, as when Cleopatra cattily wants to know the colour of the pallid Octavia's hair, or when she lies about the 'lady trifles' she squirrelled away before surrendering her treasure to Octavius. Shakespeare's language also has registers between lyrical musing and demented thunder. Consider, for example, Hamlet's brainy conceits and the fatuous euphuisms with which he mocks Osric, the barrage of adjectival insults Kent directs at Oswald in *King Lear*, the salty obscenity of the citizens in *Measure for Measure* the jargon of the financiers in *Timon of Athens*, or the bumbling officialese of Dogberry in *Much Ado*

About Nothing. The riches of Shakespearean speech are doled out equally, whether the speakers are lofty or lowly, eloquent or chatty, articulate or merely noisy. Ariel's minions in *The Tempest* vociferate by barking, crowing, or clanging like bells, Caliban is beset by apes that chatter and adders that hiss, and Stephano's four-legged monster has mouths at either end, in front to flatter and in the rear to vent curses like farts.

Through their sheer volubility, the plays demonstrate that language is our shared creation, which each of us personally reinvents. In this polyphony, the one voice we never hear is Shakespeare's own.

*

Reading Shakespeare made Gustave Flaubert feel 'greater, wiser, purer', though such a high-minded reaction leaves out of account the terror or unholy glee we may feel at performances of *Macbeth* or *A Midsummer Night's Dream*; it also ignores Shakespeare's notorious bawdry, which Ralph Waldo Emerson thought was unworthy of a 'poet-priest'. In 1947 the philosopher Emmanuel Levinas declared that his own discipline – which comprised ethics, phenomenology and ontology – amounted to 'only meditations of Shakespeare'.

Or, better yet, meditations on Shakespeare, because he does not do our thinking for us: he left intellectualizing to Hamlet, who jokes about the uninquisitive philosophy of Horatio. Nor did Shakespeare address the nation, a task he delegated to crowd-pleasers like Antony in *Julius Caesar* or Henry V. He should never be mistaken for a bard or called the Bard, which allies him with the gasbag Glendower, the Welsh magus who orates so windily in *Henry IV*. First and last, Shakespeare was a player – collaborative not prescriptive, delighting in situations that are provisional and momentary, able to simulate emotions he did not necessarily feel, and adept at the quick-witted use of words, which fabricate lies as readily as they enunciate truths.

The plays abound in mantras about the unease of crowned heads, the sweet sorrow of parting, tides and fortune, life's web and its mingled yarn, and the equation of world and stage – a store of 'practical axioms and domestic wisdom', as Samuel Johnson said. Often these homely formulations are statements of the obvious, made by people who, as Albany remarks at the end of *King Lear*, feel that something of the kind is 'what we ought to say'. Minutes before his death, Hamlet reflects that 'There is special providence in the fall of a sparrow'. This calm acceptance seems to advance beyond his earlier metaphysical disquiet – yet it is folklore, derived from the Bible. In *As You Like It* Orlando's servant Adam cheers him up by saying that God feeds the ravens and 'providently caters for the sparrow': it would be inauspicious to have the sparrow fall to the ground, as it does in Matthew's Gospel, since Adam and Orlando are on their way into exile. When Hamlet repeats the phrase, he might just be nonchalantly shrugging.

Johnson, who wanted literature to be a means of moral improvement, claimed that 'a system of civil and oeconomical prudence' could be pieced together from Shakespeare's plays. Those sayings may serve to 'patch grief', as Leonato remarks in *Much Ado About Nothing*; alternatively they can harden the heart, like the 'precepts' Coriolanus remembers Volumnia reciting to him. But such mnemonic saws do not cohere into a world-view, and they lend themselves to misuse by any opportunist. Hitler, who kept a complete Shakespeare at his eyrie outside Salzburg, adapted a remark of Hamlet's and warped its meaning. 'It is Hecuba to me,' he often said when refusing to commiserate with one or more of his victims; unlike Hamlet, who marvels at the player's simulated grief for the beleaguered queen, he was not embarrassed by his cold-bloodedness. In graver moods Hitler

Shakespeare with a sample of his philatelic wisdom.

quoted Caesar's ghostly prophecy about a meeting at Philippi, though he felt none of the guilty dread that oppresses Brutus. Quotations extracted from their dramatic context tend to bite back at those who purloin them. British politicians in Conservative governments have cited Ulysses' speech about degree from *Troilus and Cressida* and the rabble-scourging diatribes of Coriolanus as evidence that Shakespeare was a Tory. The first character is a cynic, the second a proto-fascist; the dramatist who supplies their lines takes no credit or blame for their opinions.

Like all games, the plays delight in disturbance, in taking risks and exceeding limits; sportive energy matters more than rectitude. Wyndham Lewis likened Shakespearean tragedies to rites of human sacrifice and also to bullfights: the experience is visceral, far from the purification felt by Flaubert. A set of stamps entitled 'Words of Wisdom' was issued in Gibraltar in 1998, teaming Shakespeare with Einstein, Gandhi and Winston Churchill. The physicist, the pacifist and the wartime leader had little in common, and the dramatist was an improbable adjunct. Shakespeare, like Einstein, may have made us more dangerously intelligent and more painfully sensitive but not necessarily wiser.

"Love comforts like sunshine after rain"

William Shakespeare 1564-1616

Forbidden Planet, a film released in 1956, debates the matter by launching *The Tempest* into outer space in the twenty-third century. Marooned on a remote star, its Prospero, Dr Morbius, is not an astrophysicist but a philologist – literally a lover of language, like the near-logomaniacal Shakespeare. He derives his magic from the 'almost divine race' of the extinct Krell, his predecessors on the planet, whose know-how is housed in a super-computer on 7,800 levels, 40 miles wide, that can sustain 'a whole population of creative geniuses'. Touring this cavernous engine – which is activated by electromagnetic impulses, called thoughts by earthlings – we could be inside the head of Shakespeare. The machine can materialize wishes, so it has devised Ariel and also dreamed up Caliban. Instead of a winged sprite, Morbius is served by the chunky cybernetic butler Robby the Robot, who can translate 187 languages plus their dialects and sub-tongues; the planet's 'thing of darkness' is an invisible marauding force generated by the angry id of the wise scholar. Aware of his dual capacity for both 'true creation' and destruction, Morbius refuses to take his learning back to earth aboard the flying saucer that has come to retrieve him, and instead blows up the planet. Victor Hugo, pondering a supernatural power to both create and destroy, suggested that 'Shakespeare's own tempest appalls him. It seems at times as if Shakespeare terrified Shakespeare.' The explosion at the end of the film could be one of those times.

Whether or not he was terrified, Shakespeare may have been mystified by his powers. In *The Merchant of Venice*, a lyrical diversion that passes the time while Bassanio hesitates over the caskets asks an important question about the imagination. 'Where is fancy bred, / Or in the heart, or in the head?' the singer wonders. Fancy, we're then told, is 'engender'd in the eyes', after which, being troublesome, it 'dies / In the cradle where it lies'. That puts paid to any explanation of how the plays and the people in them came about. Orsino in *Twelfth Night* is equally unhelpful. Describing his own whimsicality, he says 'So full of shapes is fancy, / That it alone is high fantastical.' The elegantly circular formulation gives nothing away. Perhaps W. H. Auden was right to suggest that Shakespeare's salvation lay in this flippancy about his own art, which differentiates him from Dante, Milton or Shaw – writers who thought they could save the world, or at least scold it into reforming itself.

'We ask and ask', as Matthew Arnold did in the sonnet he addressed to Shakespeare, but we receive no answer to our questions about his motives and purposes. Edward Bond's play *Bingo*, which imagines Shakespeare's depressed, ultimately suicidal retirement in Stratford, specifies that the 'movements and face' of the actor playing him should 'express nothing' and, in the first performances at the Royal Court in 1973, John Gielgud, usually so honey-tongued, remained almost sepulchrally silent. At one point in Bond's play, Shakespeare receives a visit from Ben Jonson who, in a moment of drunken frankness, says 'I hate you because you smile'. So much for Arnold's comment 'Thou smilest and art still'. The smile might not necessarily be genial – could it register indifference or contempt?

A brief parable by Jorge Luis Borges, entitled 'Everything and Nothing', summarizes Shakespeare's life and adds a surmise about his afterlife. Shakespeare is here seen as a paradoxical combination of plenitude and vacancy. From somewhere inside himself, Borges points out, he produced a throng of lovers, killers, kings and clowns; they had their allotted time and their allowance of sound and fury, after which, like the spirits in Prospero's pageant, they vanished. Then, depleted or perhaps repentant, Shakespeare returned to Stratford, where during the years that remained to him he counted his professional gains, topped them up with some crafty local business ventures and, as his final piece of writing, prepared the drily unliterary will in which he bequeathed to his

widow his second-best bed. But Borges was unwilling to leave it at that. Determined to penetrate the quizzical façade that intrigued Victor Hugo, consoled Matthew Arnold and alarmed Edward Bond, he speculatively follows Shakespeare into the undiscovered country and has him apologize to God for his flaws – a habit of dissimulation and a personal sense of emptiness or nonentity, the underside of his dramatic genius. Instead of responding with a rebuke or a diagnosis of multiple-personality disorder, the deity salutes the human creator, announcing 'Neither am I a single self. I dreamed the world as you dreamed your work, my Shakespeare, and you are among the shapes of my dream; like me, you are many persons and none.' God has become a fading memory, but apotheosis is no less than Shakespeare deserves.

John Gielgud as Shakespeare in *Bingo*.

World, World, O World!

A global theatre
The gods look down
Charactery
Existing, dreaming, acting

Shakespeare, like Puck, engirdles the earth: his theatre is global by both name and nature.

Vertically, its domain stretches from the upper atmosphere to the mouldering underworld. Medieval cathedrals, with their spires, their radiant stained glass, the sculpted saints clustered in their portals and the gargoyles in their guttering, were models of God's all-encompassing creation. Theatres like the Globe contained a less orderly, man-made world – not hushed by priestly protocols and, in the absence of a roof, unable to keep out the weather that soaks King Lear and tears down houses in *Macbeth*. Hamlet, in his speech about human possibility, glances at the painted ceiling of the stage and its firmament 'fretted with golden fire', a reminder of ideally elevated mental horizons, thought's skyline. But beneath the floorboards is a subliminal cellar, and in that crypt-like basement Hamlet hears the ghost of his father burrowing like a mole. Standees in the Globe's pit were called groundlings, which placed them not quite underground: the theatre's tiers were metaphysical and also social.

Horizontally, Shakespeare's stage overflows into a jostling crowd of spectators, and expands further to acknowledge the city outside the theatre. The Prologue to *Romeo and Juliet* refers to the play's 'traffic', meaning movement – of antagonistic people with combustible emotions and vaunting words, at odds in the street as the play begins. *Julius Caesar* starts with a similar affray, as citizens who ought to be at work award themselves a holiday and, like an expectant theatre audience, prepare to applaud their current favourite, a homecoming conqueror. Brutus, attempting to control his contradictory thoughts about the murder of Caesar, refers to 'the little state of man', which in its anxiety is suffering an insurrection; the theatre is just such an agitated body politic. In *Henry V* the Chorus wishes that he had 'a kingdom for a stage, princes to act'. Shakespeare fitted entire kingdoms into the Globe, and the actors who played princes – or, as at Elsinore, impersonated the king – may have assumed swanky aristocratic airs, but they were not what they pretended to be, which allowed them to suggest that none of us are. In the absence of 'monarchs to behold the swelling scene', performances could be ribald and disruptive – a demotic alternative to the drilled rigour of ceremonies at court.

Like the 'little room' in John Donne's poem 'The Good-Morrow', Shakespeare's sparsely furnished stage could be 'an everywhere'. Yet it also had a precise address, and it gave plays with antique or exotic settings a raffish local habitation in contemporary London. Stepping out of Troy at the end of *Troilus and Cressida*, Pandarus notices the 'galled' or syphilitic prostitutes in the nearby brothels of Southwark, whom he calls 'Winchester geese' because the bishop of Winchester owned land in the parish and raked in taxes from its disreputable trades. Although *Twelfth Night* is set in the illusory Balkan realm of Illyria, Antonio advises Sebastian to lodge 'in the south suburbs, at the Elephant' – an in-joke recommending an establishment very near the Globe, frequented by Shakespeare's colleagues. 'What country, friends, is this?' asks the disoriented Viola as she comes ashore at the start of the play. 'It is Illyria, lady', the sea captain replies, prompting Viola to grieve for the brother whom she believes to be in Elysium; both places are notional, equated by Viola's pun. The captain might equally well have told her 'It is the theatre, lady'. We are in a region that trips up the map-makers, located on the border between revelry and chilly reality, exempt from the laws of probability, governed by chance but open to the occasional miracle.

Shakespeare's plays often mention the name of his playhouse, with a knowing wink that emphasizes its function as a model of the world. Othello wonders why 'th' affrighted globe' does not lay on a solar and lunar eclipse to magnify his disaster. The 'wooden O' strains to find room for naval fleets and battlefields in *Henry V*, and it dilates even further to accommodate Falstaff, whose physical size and dexterous mental range make him, as Hal says in *Henry IV*, a 'globe of sinful continents'. Hamlet vows to heed the ghost's command so long as 'memory holds a seat / In this distracted globe': he is referring to his encyclopaedic but somewhat addled head.

Despite its cosmic symbolism, the open-air platform had its limitations, which Shakespeare ingeniously exceeds. The Chorus in *Henry V* apologizes for restricted space and limited personnel, and asks us to compensate by dividing one man 'into a thousand parts' and imagining that we can see an army. At the sheep-shearing festival in *The Winter's Tale* Florizel performs a converse feat with words alone. He multiplies one man into mankind by broadcasting his love for Perdita to Polixenes, then to Camillo, and so on indefinitely to 'more / Than he; and men, the earth, the heavens, and all'. The same grandiloquent gesture is repeated with a sharper edge by Paulina when she upbraids Leontes for mistreating his dead wife. He could not restore Hermione, she says,

> If, one by one, you wedded all the world,
> Or from the all that are took something good.

Given world enough and time, Leontes might make the experiment: this all-embracing universality is the instinct of Shakespearean drama. No single individual ever monopolizes his stage, as the warlord in Marlowe's *Tamburlaine the Great* insists on doing. Minor characters are the protagonists of personal dramas that they may not have the chance to act out. Hence the aside with which the hapless Sir Andrew Aguecheek in *Twelfth Night* testifies that he 'was adored once too'. People who remain subdued or silent can claim our attention when we see them on stage: what misgivings might Jessica have at the end of *The Merchant of Venice*, after being carried off to Belmont by the Christians who ruined her father?

Conviviality has to combat solipsism. 'Now I am alone' says Hamlet, relieved that the courtiers have departed. But his habit of soliloquizing belies his gregarious nature: the stage is a plenum, crowded like a public street even if, as at the end of *Richard II*, the only person on it is a prisoner in his cell. Aware that 'the world is populous', Richard touchingly creates a psychodrama to fill up his enclosure. He sets his male soul and female brain to 'beget / A generation of still-breeding thoughts' that then engage in an internecine war, cancel each other out, and restore him to solitude. 'I… straight am nothing,' he concludes. A play by Shakespeare likewise brings people together, then either leaves them for dead or sends them away to separate futures. This assembly and dispersal happen both on the stage and off it. We arrive as strangers, form a community inside the theatre, then afterwards are thrust back into a reality we may have forgotten about. In the epilogue to *As You Like It* Rosalind softens that enforced exit by ingratiating with the women in the audience while simultaneously flirting with the men and requesting our thanks for her 'kind offer'. At the end of *Love's Labour's Lost*, Armado is more curt. 'You that way, we this way,' he says as he points us towards the door.

Tragedies, paradoxically, let us down more gently than these comedies do: usually, after the hero's death, appropriate arrangements are made for the obsequies. Fortinbras says that Hamlet 'was likely, had he been put on, / To have proved most royal', which adroitly covers his annexation of the Danish throne. Somewhat more crassly, Lodovico in *Othello* tells Gratiano to 'seize upon the fortunes of the Moor / For they succeed on you'. As well as settling matters of inheritance, the survivors in tragedy worry about continuity, which means sustaining and renewing what Albany in *King Lear* calls 'the gored state'. In the comedies, a happy ending is not guaranteed to all. Malvolio in *Twelfth Night* stalks off to plan revenge, and Jaques in *As You Like It* refuses to take a partner, says he is not 'for dancing measures', and retreats to the Duke's 'abandoned cave', now his misanthropic hermitage.

The
Chronicle Hiftory
of
Henry the Fift
with his battel
fought at
Agin Court
in France

The Spanish dramatist Pedro Calderón de la Barca also set his staged allegories in what he called 'the great theatre of the world'. In 1653 in *El Gran Teatro del Mundo*, Calderón's God supervises the terrestrial panorama, studying the actors to determine their posthumous destination; the creator, otherwise known as the Author, has supreme authority. Perhaps luckily, Shakespeare's characters are not the subjects of a divine puppeteer. 'Wherefore was I born?' asks Bolingbroke in *Richard II*. The question concerns his inherited rights, but it has a more plaintive underside, and there is no presiding author to resolve his existential doubts or certify his uniqueness. In a comfortlessly secular lament, Edgar in *King Lear* cries 'World, world, O world!' as he meets his outcast father, a victim of the 'strange mutations' that afflict us all. That exclamation, varied elsewhere, is almost a refrain. 'I hold the world but as the world', says the depressed Antonio in *The Merchant of Venice*; despite Portia's sermon, no mercy rains down on him from heaven, and he has to be saved from Shylock's knife by a legalistic trick. In despair, Leontes in *The Winter's Tale* decides that 'the world and all that's in't is nothing', as temporary as a theatrical show. Are we 'merely players', as Jaques in *As You Like It* puts it when he elaborates his metaphor of the world as a stage? Happily, his adverb is not as disparaging as it sounds: for Shakespeare, 'merely' meant 'primarily'. Our world-stage is self-sufficient; we perform for one another, not to audition for the afterlife. In Emilio de' Cavalieri's metaphysical oratorio *Rappresentatione di Anima, e di Corpo*, performed in Florence in 1600, a character called Mondo brags of his corpulent abundance. Like a play by Shakespeare, he is the sum total of everything that exists, both good and bad.

Looking skywards, transactions with the gods or with God seldom go well for Shakespeare's suppliants. Leontes' abused wife Hermione trusts that 'powers divine / Behold our human actions'. She adds 'as they do', but her afterthought leaves open the possibility that they perhaps do not. Titus Andronicus sends urgent messages to Olympus by firing arrows at the sky; his letters are not answered. Coriolanus expects to hear mocking laughter from above when the assembled deities see him capitulate to his mother. Gods sometimes descend in machines, as in the classical theatre, although they are not always treated respectfully. Hymen in *As You Like It* appears by arrangement with the obscure magician whom Rosalind claims as an acquaintance. The gossipy goddesses in the wedding masque at the end of *The Tempest* are sent packing when Prospero remembers that he has other business to attend to. Jupiter swoops down on an eagle in *Cymbeline*, and Sicilius sniffs the 'sulphurous' odour of his 'celestial breath'; Cymbeline, sacrificing to the gods, prays that the smoke from the altar will make its way to 'their nostrils', which treats the Olympians as creatures with human bodies who just happen to be immortal.

Judgement is likewise olfactory for Claudius in *Hamlet*, who says that his crime is rank and 'smells to heaven'. Does God find his creatures odious? Or do we dismay higher powers, rather than disgusting them? Isabella in *Measure for Measure* imagines the angels weeping at the misbehaviour of man, who when seen from above looks like 'an angry ape'. Apes are mimics: the phrase registers the starchy nun's contempt for our tawdry emotionalism, and also for actors who trade in counterfeit passions. When Angelo in the same play likens the snooping Duke to 'power divine', he is not deferring to Calderón's Author. Instead the smarmy comment externalizes Angelo's uneasy conscience; it also flatters the Duke's sanctimonious self-conceit. Prince John in *Henry IV* calls the archbishop of York 'the imagin'd voice of God Himself' or 'the speaker in His parliament', but he does so sarcastically. Parliament, like a play by Shakespeare, is a contentious babble, with no megaphonic divine adjudicator to control the hubbub.

Only the personification of Time in *The Winter's Tale* escapes such agnostic irony. Time's role is to mediate between a tragedy in the first part of the play and the comedy that, after an interval of sixteen years, succeeds it. To do so is to solve the riddle of literature – to find common ground between the two dramatic genres that classical theory declared incompatible, and to explain as well why the world, as Time says, contains 'both joy and terror'. Tragedy foreshortens time by having young Mamillius die so prematurely; then, in the seasonal revelry of rural Bohemia, comedy demonstrates that time is unending, cyclical, annually repetitious. But does time heal wounds, as we are told when we lose loved ones, or does it merely slide over grief by leading us to forgetfulness with 'swift passage'? In its speech, Time vows to please some, but threatens to 'try all': our existence from day to day, decade to decade, is a trial, a stress test. Time qualifies for this commanding choral role because it is the medium of our mortality. A physical force rather than a figure expecting to be worshipped, it is the one true god in Shakespeare's plays. Hamlet refers to 'a divinity that shapes our ends' and tidies up what we have left rough and ragged; Viola in *Twelfth Night* expresses a similar wish when she says

O time, thou must untangle this, not I.
It is too hard a knot for me to untie.

In *The Winter's Tale*, Time claims no such shapely aesthetic powers and promises no neat denouements. It has authority because it conducts each of us to our end, determining when we will die while making sure that the globe continues to spin, unscathed by our absence.

*

In a counterpart to Calderón's theatrical allegory, Lear sees the world as a 'great stage of fools', where kings forfeit their privileges, clowns sometimes function as sages, and bad weather enforces the pitiful vulnerability that equalizes them. 'What is the cause of thunder?' Lear asks: surely not divine ire. Stranded in his own 'little world of man', he challenges the storm to flatten 'the thick rotundity o' th' world'. Thanks to the simple, magnificently eloquent adjective 'thick', the small planet that is lashed by the elements and by his rhetoric remains indestructible. Shakespeare's world is densely packed, as is Lear's phrase with its abbreviated monosyllables; its roundness recalls the obese kitchen maid Dowsabel in *The Comedy of Errors*, who is 'spherical, like a globe' and is so boosted by Dromio of Syracuse's description – her buttocks represent boggy Ireland, her teeth resemble England's chalk cliffs, her hot breath reeks of Spain, and her lower extremities constitute the Netherlands – that she cannot be squeezed onstage. A world this bulky, stuffed with men and women of all kinds, is not little after all, and it will never be deflated.

Surveying the newcomers to Prospero's island with a naïvely wondering gaze, Miranda says 'How many goodly creatures are there here! How beauteous mankind is!' For her, this new world is 'brave': it has bravura, it dazzles, since those beauteous beings – in truth a disreputable lot, and mostly far from admirable – must have been fashioned by a wizard like her father. Hamlet too praises the species to which he belongs, even though our god-like mental capacity depends on a body that is doomed to decompose. Posturing, he claims that 'Man delights not me', then changes his mind when told that the players are on their way. The news provokes him to summon up a cast of supplementary selves to perform his psychodrama: the adventurous knight, the lover, the humorous man (as neurotic as Hamlet himself), the clown, and the lady who is actually a boy. Such caricatures befit a *commedia dell'arte*, but Shakespeare's theatre frames the proud self-presentation of more upright, autonomous specimens, closer to Hamlet's humanist ideal. 'You see me, Lord Bassanio, where I stand, / Such as I am', says Portia in *The Merchant of Venice*. Othello refuses to hide from Brabantio, and says 'My parts, my title, and my perfect soul / Shall manifest me rightly'. 'Here is my space,' declares Antony, fixing on Alexandria as the centre of his world and at the same time asserting his command of the stage. 'Kingdoms are clay', he adds: political realms lack the solidity of the boards he bestrides.

At the start of *Cymbeline*, a courtier extols Posthumus for possessing 'so fair an outward and such stuff within'. He then apologizes because this seems to 'crush him together rather than unfold / His measure duly'. Macbeth says something similar in reverse order, and with a darker intent. He tells his wife that he has 'strange things… in head', but his desires 'must be acted ere they may be scann'd'. He will only know who he is when he sees what actions he is capable of performing. These are the complementary ways in which Shakespeare's people come alive – outwardly unfolded in dramatic action, revealed within by poetic speech; overheard as they mentally rehearse, then exposed to view as they step into the public domain and perform the actions they have dreamed about or try out the identities they have devised.

'Fellow,' demands Claudio in *Measure for Measure* as a jailer hauls him through the streets, 'why dost thou show me thus to the world?' Cleopatra too dreads being exhibited, mocked by 'quick comedians' in Rome who 'will stage us' when they 'present / Our Alexandrian revels'. Malvolio in *Twelfth Night* is enticed into travestying himself when he appears cross-gartered, and the hidden tormenters who spy on his preening antics goad us to enjoy the spectacle. But the intention is not only punitive, as Claudio and Cleopatra assume. As well as looking at Malvolio, we hear his private thoughts as he reads the letter that has encouraged him to imagine making love to Olivia. That breach ought to complicate our reaction: how can we not feel guilty for laughing, since we surely dread being tricked into the same self-betrayal? From outside, Malvolio looks comic. Inside, he is potentially tragic – insecure, touchy, easily damaged or destroyed. Ours is a double perspective, watching from an amused distance like Maria and Sir Toby but also intimately participating in the fantasy life of their victim.

Touchstone in *As You Like It* says that 'the truest poetry is the most feigning'; actors are even truer feigners, habitual pretenders. Denis Diderot, who met Garrick in 1765, marvelled at his capacity to change his expression from joy to cheerfulness to serenity to dejection to terror, feeling none of the emotions sketched by his face. In Shakespeare, what Diderot called 'the paradox of the actor' is subtler, more psychologically and behaviourally complex than mere fakery. The plays suggest that we are truest to ourselves when we are most artful, since we all conceal meanings in an unspoken subtext and hide behind personae.

The characters in *Macbeth* have their own devious version of Diderot's paradox. At the English court, Malcolm claims to be a rapacious traitor, extravagantly accusing himself of atrocities to test Macduff's 'good truth and honour'. The feint is too elaborate and too vivid to be entirely imaginary: if he can describe a career of debauchery in such gloating detail, then he is surely capable of 'acting it many ways', and there is no reason for Macduff to trust him when he unspeaks his self-condemnation and reveals 'what I am truly'. Macduff then discovers that his wife and children have been murdered, and is told by Malcolm to control his grief. 'I must also feel it like a man', he replies, but instead of emoting he boasts of a merely theatrical facility – 'I could play the woman with mine eyes / And braggart with my tongue!' – after which he arranges the implacable face that is appropriate for an avenger. 'This tune goes manly', says Malcolm, pleased by Macduff's rhetorical shift. Was Lady Macduff right to think her husband unfeeling when he left her in harm's way? 'He wants the natural touch', she says shortly before her death: he was merely acting the roles of husband and father.

Macbeth bears 'a charmèd life', and believes that the witches have made him unkillable; in fact the charm belongs to the technical armature of actors, who never have to die in earnest. Macduff breaks through this protective cladding because he is not 'of woman born', having been 'from his mother's womb / Untimely ripped': his Caesarean birth has spared him from trauma and made him impervious to pain, which turns him into an efficient killer. Acting for these men is a kind of anaesthesia, a professionally useful dehumanization.

Yet beneath their layers of artifice, Shakespeare's characters still persuade us that, like Hamlet, they 'have that within which passeth show'. When they talk to themselves we eavesdrop on consciousness, and because the mind is a physical organ we track thoughts that race with crackling immediacy along internal networks. In decline, Antony brags that his brain still 'nourishes our nerves', and sees the competition between brown and grey hairs on his scalp as a sign of enduring vigour. The emotions that agitate these people are an internal weather, balmy or tempestuous. Enobarbus likens Cleopatra's sighs and tears to atmospheric effusions, attuned to the love-sick winds and amorously lapping waters that buoy up her barge; the lachrymose Juliet, as her father complains, resembles 'a barque, a sea, a wind', kept afloat by her weeping and wailing. Bodies can hardly withstand the 'thousand natural shocks' that, as Hamlet says, besiege our flesh. Macbeth feels his 'seated heart knock at my ribs', almost dislodged as it rattles his stalwart frame. After Gloucester's supposed fall from the cliff in *King Lear*, Edgar says that even if he had been made of 'gossamer, feathers, air', he should have shattered when he hit the ground. Instead, as he tells the frail old man, 'thou… / Hast heavy substance'. The phrase is a law of physics and a moral admonition:

the body, like the life it houses, is a burden we must carry for as long as we can.

We have to decide for ourselves why Edgar cast his father in this tragicomic playlet, which looks like a vindictive jest. He remains inscrutable, which is the norm in Shakespeare. Unlike the omniscient narrators of novels, dramatists can offer no elucidation in the margins; Shakespeare's characters must interpret their actions themselves, if they can – which means that actors have to invent backstories or research psychoanalytical theories to arrive at some convenient diagnosis. Iago is unsure why he detests Othello, and gives a variety of reasons, none of which seems to convince him. Oliver in *As You Like It* says that his soul loathes his brother Orlando, 'yet I know not why'. The very notion of a motive could be a misnomer: it implies that we possess some internal switch that turns our motors on.

It may even be wrong to think of these people as characters, like the heroines whose conduct is examined and explicated by Jane Austen and George Eliot. For Shakespeare, the word 'character' is at best a metaphor. It refers to lettering, as in the 'characters of brass' the Duke refers to in *Measure for Measure*, or the 'glitt'ring golden characters' that spell out Marina's epitaph in *Pericles*; applied to human beings, it carries with it the delusion of legibility. In *The Two Gentlemen of Verona* Julia calls Lucetta 'the table wherein all my thoughts / Are visibly character'd and engrav'd, / To lesson me'. Character here is entabulated, like the maxim about smiling villainy that Hamlet wants to transcribe in his 'tables' or notebook. Incised as well, more indelible than writing, it seeks to document traits that are permanent and morally sound. Lady Macbeth has her own duplicitous version of Julia's image. Macbeth's face, she tells him, is 'as a book where men / May read strange matters', with luck encrypted and thus safe from detection or decipherment. Better that than the transparency of Morton in *Henry IV*, whose forehead Northumberland likens to 'a title leaf' that 'foretells the nature of a tragic volume'. Brutus in *Julius Caesar* promises to share with Portia his political secrets, translating the 'charactery of my sad brows'; nevertheless he orders her to 'Leave me with haste' and remains unreadable.

Shakespeare usually presents us with illegible characters – people who are mutable, malleable, shedding name, class and even gender as easily as clothing. 'Edgar I nothing am,' says Gloucester's son; he next appears as a gibbering beggar and is unrecognizable. 'Uncase thee,' says Lucentio to Tranio in *The Taming of the Shrew*: master and servant then swap clothes, as do Antony and Cleopatra when she dresses him in her 'tires and mantles' before she buckles on his sword to swagger around the bedroom. Orlando, protecting old Adam in the forest, calls himself a doe with a faun to feed. 'Unsex me here', Lady Macbeth begs the spirits who minister to her dreams of power as she limbers up to kill. More casually, Pisanio in *Cymbeline* tells Imogen that to save herself she 'must forget to be a woman', and she responds that she is 'almost / A man already'. The hyphenated 'master-mistress of my passion' in the twentieth sonnet blends the sexes or alternates between them without needing to adopt a disguise. A later sonnet assails those who treat their emotions as an asset that cannot be spent, acting as 'lords and owners of their faces'. 'Unmoved, cold', even while they are 'moving others', these guarded, self-possessed creatures could never take part in one of Shakespeare's plays, where people have to be fluid, perpetually mobile, ready to metamorphose at a moment's notice. Identity – which derives from the Latin 'idem' and therefore wants people to be always the same – is perhaps something we are better off without.

The tragic and comic masks of classical drama sorted people into categories by fixing facial expressions in a rictus, with a mouth either turned down at the corners or grinning inanely. Shakespeare superimposes those façades. Claudius in *Hamlet*, a politician and thus a talented actor, balances 'an auspicious and a dropping eye', displaying gaiety and gravity on opposite sides of his flexible face. Antonio in *The Merchant of Venice* feels sad without knowing why, which makes him a tragic figure stranded in a comedy; trying to understand his friend's melancholy, Solanio swears 'by two-headed Janus' that 'Nature hath framed strange fellows in her time'. The most Janus-faced incidents in Shakespeare's plays are reported by witnesses, almost as if actors cannot be trusted to represent such an amalgam of emotions. We are told that 'joy waded in tears' during the reunion of Leontes and Perdita in *The Winter's Tale*, and that Gloucester's heart '"Twixt two extremes of passion, joy and grief, / Burst smilingly' as he undramatically sat under a tree. Hence too the meteorological description of Cordelia's emotions when she receives news of Lear: her face shows 'sunshine and rain at once', the mixed weather of tragicomedy.

Our reaction to such reports is a test of solicitude, and the plays remind us that we can choose which mask to wear. Perhaps, like Bassanio teasing his Venetian friends, we ask 'When shall we laugh? Say, when?' Those of us with 'vinegar aspect' refuse to show our teeth in response to a jest; others, like Gratiano when he tries to cheer up Antonio, allow mirth to line their faces prematurely with 'old wrinkles'. Miranda experiences the tempest as a personal trauma, and says 'O, I have suffered / With those that I saw suffer!' Prospero too is stung into compassion when Ariel tells him that even he would pity the distracted courtiers, 'were I human'. The subjunctive mood of that phrase is a challenge to us as well as to Prospero. Ariel's skill in whipping up the scenic effects of the storm has turned disaster into spectacle, like the player at Elsinore who re-enacts Hecuba's despair 'in a fiction, in a dream of passion'. Rather than admiring the sprite's technical sorcery, we are impelled to care about the needless agonies of the people on the ship, and unless we do so, the world is at risk of turning out to be a fragile bubble, a container for nothing but Prospero's 'air... thin air'.

*

Life and performance are often equated in Shakespeare's plays. The point is made sardonically by Jaques as he traverses the ages of man, sheepishly by Puck in his farewell, and nihilistically by Prospero when he interrupts the masque. Could our supposed reality be a charade, a mock-up that deceives and then disillusions us? The theatre, as Prospero warns, is where we see towers, palaces and temples toppling – as they do in Colman's *The Edge of Doom* – after which perhaps 'the great globe itself... shall dissolve'. Shakespeare juggles creation and destruction, just as his people invent and revise or efface themselves before our eyes.

Borges suggested that Shakespeare wrote in a 'controlled hallucination'. That suits the action of *A Midsummer Night's Dream*, in which Theseus likens love and poetry to lunacy and derives all three from 'seething brains' that deal in 'shaping fantasies'. Puck's accident-prone magic results in violent mischief, but he offers only a perfunctory apology for the play's mayhem. Prospero at least prays for forgiveness after his 'so potent art' shakes the earth, uproots trees, and hauls the dead from their graves. Puck merely recommends that, if we are offended by what we have seen, we should pretend that we half-slumbered through the play, which makes it our hallucination.

In the comedies, that hypothesis often explains away a disordered reality. At the end of *The Taming of the Shrew*, the swinish Sly grumbles about being woken from 'the best dream / That ever I had in my life', a vindication of male dominance that has been performed on his behalf by the wife-beating Petruchio. 'Are all the people mad?' cries Sebastian in *Twelfth Night*, irritated, infuriated and – when Olivia wraps him in an embrace after first setting eyes on him – entranced by Illyria. Antipholus of Syracuse attributes the farcical mix-ups in *The Comedy of Errors* to

> nimble jugglers, that deceive the eye,
> Dark-working sorcerers, that change the mind,
> Soul-killing witches, that deform the body.

The Duke, seeing Antipholus and his twin together, suggests that 'One of these men is genius to the other'. Genius here means a spirit whose function is to grant wishes, although in other cases no supernatural aid is necessary. 'Prove true, imagination, O prove true,' says Viola when she first suspects that Sebastian may be alive. Charmian in *Antony and Cleopatra* asks the soothsayer how many children she will bear, and he replies 'If every of your wishes had a womb, / And fertile every wish, a million' – a prolific bodily equivalent to the offspring of restless thoughts enumerated by Richard II in his cell.

Such wish-fulfilling acts of imagination sometimes turn the action we watch into what Strindberg called a 'dream play'. Brooding about the plan to kill Caesar, Brutus reflects that 'the acting of a dreadful thing' is preceded by a mental rehearsal that is 'like a phantasma or a hideous dream': almost cinematically, he projects an image of himself into the future and watches it commit the proscribed deed on his behalf. Othello accepts Iago's made-up story about Cassio's talking in his sleep as evidence of Desdemona's infidelity, and is not dissuaded even when Iago challenges his credulity by ironically warning 'Nay, this was but his dream'. Othello calls the fictitious reverie 'a foregone conclusion', as if we can only dream about something that has already occurred or will inevitably do so in the future. He also forgets that he has asked for 'ocular proof', whereas Iago is at best an ear-witness.

Macbeth's crimes originate as what he calls 'horrible imaginings', and even on the battlefield he is complimented for making 'strange images of death'. He envisions a 'dagger of the mind', described by his wife as 'an air-drawn dagger'. The play's corpses are conjured up by poetry. Macdonwald is 'unseam'd... from the nave to th' chops', surgically opened not butchered – or is the suture that parts him from the navel to the jaw like stitching in a fabric, undoing sleep's capacity to knit up 'the ravell'd sleeve of care', as Macbeth puts it in one of his finicky, feminine metaphors? Just as incongruously, Macbeth sees Duncan's 'silver skin laced with his golden blood': precious metals aestheticize gore, and 'laced' adds an extra decorative frill. Later, in the same excessive or lushly extravagant spirit, a hired thug reports that he left Banquo with 'twenty trenchèd gashes on his head, / The least a death to nature', which surely counts as overkill.

Lady Macbeth is also capable of wildly fantasizing, as she does when she imagines killing an infant as it suckles her. She cannot know 'how tender 'tis to love that babe that milks me', since the Macbeths are childless; the outrage is an exercise, designed to goad Macbeth into action. As actors do, she incites a feeling by retrieving what she claims is a personal memory, and relies on language to give the situation its physical reality: the earthiness of 'I have given suck', the unhurtful adhesion of the 'boneless gums' attached to her nipple, her sudden and disgusted view of the baby as a parasitical feeder on her body that she has the right to exterminate, and her vicious insistence that she would smash its squashy head while it was 'smiling in my face'. The creative thinking with which she fills out the scene of destruction is exactly what Borges attributed to Shakespeare, whose expertise at entering the minds and bodies of others demonstrates 'the fundamental identity of existing, dreaming, and acting'.

A hallucination is a mental mirage, seen by a poetic eye that, as Theseus puts it, is 'in fine frenzy rolling'. Leonardo da Vinci considered the human eye to be more admirable than 'all other things created by God' because it could compress the world in its moist globe and 'conduct man to all corners of the universe'.

Thanks to the 'vile jelly' that is torn from its sockets in *King Lear*, Shakespeare's characters send themselves on such journeys beyond the horizon. As Posthumus sails into banishment in *Cymbeline*, Imogen indulges in a wide-ranging ocular adventure, her own extravagant feat of image-making. Cracking her 'eyestrings', she tracks her husband until he diminishes to a needle-point or melts 'from / The smallness of a gnat to air'; then, she says, she will retract those telescopic organs, restore them to her face, and use them for weeping. The same circle closes in the narrative poem *Venus and Adonis*, where the eyes of Venus look away from the slain Adonis and withdraw 'into the deep-dark cabins of her head' like a snail that 'shrinks backward in his shelly cave'. Some of Shakespeare's most curious, questing metaphors probe that recess, where dreams and poetic images are hatched. Spying on Imogen as she sleeps, Iachimo watches the candle flame attempt to

> under-peep her lids,
> To see th' enclosed lights, now canopied
> Under those windows, white and azure lac'd
> With blue of heaven's own tint.

With creepy rapture he trespasses behind her closed eyes and inscribes his own fantasy on the internal sky of her drowsy mind.

The scenarios dreamed up by all those inflamed imaginations makes Shakespeare's plays seem – as the Poet says when he flatters the Painter's canvases in *Timon of Athens* – 'livelier than life'. His remarks apply to acting, even in a dumb show:

> What a mental power
> This eye shoots forth! How big imagination
> Moves in this lip!

Life means being lively, which is why Hamlet describes death as a 'fell sergeant' who is 'strict in his arrest': to be arrested is to be halted, stopped in your tracks, and for Hamlet, who twice tells Horatio 'I am dead' while he goes on talking, immobility is a premonition of the silence that will soon follow. As the Poet implies in *Timon*, forms that are either pictorially flat or statuesque and marmoreal only appeal when they stir into animation. Cleopatra is sarcastically pleased to be told that her staid rival Octavia 'shows a body rather than a life; / A statue, than a breather'. But in *Venus and Adonis* the goddess has no interest in merely aesthetic values, and upbraids the bashful youth as a

> lifeless picture, cold and senseless stone,
> Well painted idol, image dun and dead,
> Statue contenting but the eye alone.

Paulina says that the effigy of Hermione shows 'life as lively mock'd as ever / Still sleep mock'd death', which adds a sad qualification to the Poet's compliment in *Timon*. Then the figure steps down from its pedestal and speaks, which forces us to redraw the boundaries between art and nature, representation and reincarnation.

The end of *Cymbeline* also disentangles the plot by bringing back the dead, though it does so more frantically than *The Winter's Tale*. Posthumus wildly pleads for his own execution after accusing himself of having Imogen killed. She appears, self-exhumed; he knocks her down, believing her to be an imposter, and in effect kills her again. She revives a second time, as her father wonders if 'the gods do mean to strike me / To death with mortal joy'. Posthumus complains of the 'staggers'; Cymbeline asks 'Does the world go round?' It does, and Shakespeare's plays accelerate that rotation. 'Man', as Benedick puts it after reversing himself in *Much Ado About Nothing*, 'is a giddy thing, and this is my conclusion'.

The actual conclusion will arrive somewhat later, when

> thoughts, the slaves of life, and life, time's fool,
> And time, that takes survey of all the world,
> Must have a stop.

Although Hotspur in *Henry IV* dies seconds after uttering those words, he says 'must' not 'will': he is speaking theoretically, and the eschatological last things remain a matter of conjecture. On his way to the end of the sentence, Hotspur acknowledges that time is engaged in a leisurely, almost stately enterprise that cannot be interrupted: it 'takes survey of all the world'. Here is another aerial glimpse of the globe, with time overseeing and mapping space, and a poignant parting glance at a man who after so much heroic bluster now quietly takes note of his insignificant death, which occurs at time's pleasure because life, seen from the viewpoint of eternity, is a laughing matter. With his last breath, Hotspur sums up the grand, panoptic vision of Shakespeare.

A Piece of Work

When Lear sees the wretched, raving Poor Tom, he asks 'Is man no more than this?' That vexing question recurs throughout Shakespeare's plays: they exist to provoke it, and they leave the answer up to us. The theatre is where we go to scrutinize ourselves.

As a humanist, Hamlet assumes that culture has perfected nature, which is why he calls man 'a piece of work'. His accolade – partly aesthetic, partly spiritual – explains why Miranda finds mankind beauteous. For Hamlet, human beings count as 'the beauty of the world' and are 'in apprehension… like a god'. 'Infinite in faculty', we are all the same sculpted from dust, so the workmanship of our maker is open to question. Is man, in truth, much less than this? 'The paragon of animals' declines into debility when Hamlet mocks old men with gummed-up eyes and weak hams; Yorick's head, once full of 'excellent fancy', is excavated by worms.

Concentrating on this mismatch between the winged mind and the hobbled body, Shakespeare invented a new kind of drama – more attentive to the contraries of actual existence than medieval morality plays, which dealt with the soul's journey towards salvation; remote as well from the stark simplicity of classical tragedy, with its emphasis on decisive, usually fatal action.

According to Aristotle, the theatre studied irreversible choices: Agamemnon stepping on to the red carpet, the meeting at the crossroads that determines the future of Oedipus. Activity, in Aristotle's view, was the purpose of existence, and drama followed this trajectory; there was no need to bother with the personal qualities or characteristics of the cautionary figures whose fate the plays studied. But Shakespeare's stage belongs to his exuberant people, for whom it is, as Hamlet says of the earth, a 'goodly frame'. No fatal divine decrees constrain them. Cleopatra entertains us with her 'infinite variety'; Richard III, a one-man variety show, likens himself to slippery Proteus and to the chameleon with its changeful chromatic skin; Mercutio exists to be mercurial. Although Hamlet's hymn of praise specifies that man is 'in action… like an angel', Shakespeare's great characters are often luxuriantly inactive, absorbed by contemplation of their own complexity. Hamlet accuses himself of Lethean laziness and of not deserving 'the name of action'; Falstaff is idle on principle. On the heath in *King Lear* or in the forest in *As You Like It*, people spend the time exchanging ideas about who and where they are: in the tragedy they conduct a mock trial, in the comedy they play amorous games, until a summons from offstage mobilizes them and re-activates the stationary plot.

Whereas Aristotle insisted on the opposition between the speed of drama and the expansive leisure of narrative, we are happy to watch these people sit on the ground, as Richard II proposes, to tell their sad or merry stories, because the tragicomic predicament they discuss is ours as well. Richard speaks of 'the hollow crown / That rounds the mortal temples of a king', although – contradicting the classical emphasis on great men – this is not an exclusively royal plight. Every human being wears a hollow, temporary diadem until decay, germinating within, demolishes those temples and mocks the word we use to make our heads sacrosanct.

'Who is it that can tell me who I am?' asks Lear. Identity depends on our 'lendings', the grubby rags or expensive furs that hide us; underneath we are dress dummies, lay figures, like actors before they put on their costumes. 'Unbutton here,' Lear cries in his derangement, and before he dies he asks again for help undoing another button. Clothes offend him because they are disguises, stolen from more ingenuous creatures: Poor Tom, by contrast, owes 'the worm no silk, the beast no hide, the sheep no wool'. Kent presses the idea further when he scorns the lackey Oswald, sneering that 'nature disclaims in thee. A tailor made thee.' It is more than a joke: Shakespeare's plays speculate about

our creation or manufacture, and take people to pieces without being sure that they can be put together again.

Orson Welles once said that actors should be regarded as 'neither men nor women' and assigned to 'a third sex'; he even suggested that his colleagues were 'crooks' – as deceitful as politicians, who also spend their careers acting. This chuckling raillery articulates a worry voiced by many characters in the plays. Duncan, betrayed by the Thane of Cawdor, regrets that 'There's no art / To find the mind's construction in the face'. Acting ought to be such an art, but as well as making the mind visible it protects us from surveillance by reconstructing facial expressions. A visage is a visor, a means of self-defence. Hamlet rails against cosmetics; in *Twelfth Night*, when Olivia unveils a countenance she describes as 'the picture', Viola sceptically comments that it is 'excellently done, if God made all'. Richard III brags that he can 'counterfeit the deep tragedian', which may be what Hamlet is doing with his inky cloak and his woeful demeanour as he ostentatiously mourns his father.

A mid-nineteenth century procession of Shakespearean characters, including Crab the dog, formerly attributed to Daniel Maclise.

The Fool, answering Lear's question, tells him that he is 'Lear's shadow' – the flattened outline of a body that blocks the light; perhaps also a player insanely convinced that he is or once was a king. Actors function as our shadow selves, avatars who, as the psychiatrist Jung said, 'make the darkness conscious'. Shakespeare holds a mirror up to nature, as Hamlet says, but can we trust what it shows us, or trust ourselves to recognize our own feigning faces?

*

At the end of *Julius Caesar*, Antony pays tribute to Brutus by saying that the elements were so equably blended in him that 'Nature might stand up / And say to all the world "This was a man."' The commendation sounds shiftily impersonal, and frigidly un-Shakespearean as well: there is no chemical recipe for concocting a human being, and if what matters is mixing the correct proportions of earth, air, fire and water then we should all be uniform, and drama, which is generated by our dissimilarities, would not exist.

Antony gives too much credit to the goddess extolled by Lucretius, whose treatise *De Rerum Natura* was rediscovered in the sixteenth century. The nature that Hamlet wants the mirror to reflect may be a human invention, defined by each of us to suit ourselves. Antony for instance calls Brutus 'gentle' – gentlemanly, which is what Duncan says of the treacherous Cawdor, or merely well-bred? – although that makes it difficult to explain the unkind cut that felled Caesar. Hector in *Troilus and Cressida* tells more of the truth about the inherited or innate muddle of our making. He is obliged to fight Ajax, who happens to be his 'father's sister's son, / A cousin-german'. Their 'commixtion' makes it impossible for either of them to say which of their arms or legs is a 'Greekish member' and which is Trojan; this uncertainty results in a convenient stalemate, as Hector refuses to raise his sword against a part of himself. We like to think we are individuals, meaning that we are indivisible, but both physically and mentally each of us is an assemblage, a sort of Greekish and Trojan hybrid. For this reason, in one of Shakespeare's oddest yet most wrenching scenes, Imogen in *Cymbeline* mistakes the decapitated corpse of the foul Cloten for her beloved Posthumus. Doting on what is left of him, she enumerates the godly or heroic provenance of parts – a foot Mercurial, a Martial thigh, Herculean brawn – that, in the head's absence, do not add up into a whole. If people are interchangeable, as the Romans in *Julius Caesar* want to be, it is only from the neck down.

After Cleopatra has loosened his rectitude, Antony makes amends for the formulaic view of nature expressed in his elegy for Brutus. At the party on Pompey's galley in *Antony and Cleopatra*, his fellow triumvirs want to know 'what manner o' thing' the Egyptian crocodile is. Antony, befuddled by drink, can only say that 'It is shaped… like itself; and it is as broad as it hath breadth: it is just so high as it is, and moves with it own organs.' His fumbling is inadvertently truthful: aren't we all equally idiosyncratic?

Lucretius pointed out that nature is playful, forever devising new varieties of life; the same is true of Shakespeare. Ben Jonson even snidely accused him of inventing creatures unlike any in the world around us and making 'nature afraid' of his 'drolleries'. Jonson might have had in mind the mutants encountered by Othello, since he suggests that it was Shakespeare's habit 'to mix his head with other men's heels'. Renaissance artists, however, were proud of such mould-breaking novelties: Leonardo da Vinci believed that painters practised a noble, liberal art because they could depict 'infinite things that nature never created'.

Antony adds a postscript about the crocodile's afterlife, which again draws on the Aristotelian theory that he employs when he praises Brutus. 'The elements once out of it,' he says of the monster, 'it transmigrates.' So do many Shakespearean characters. Bottom's overnight translation into an ass makes possible his perverse but rapturous tryst with the fairy queen, and next morning he is grateful for the bottomless strangeness of what he decides was a dream. Gratiano cites the Pythagorean doctrine of metempsychosis – the belief that consciousness can commute between species – as an excuse for persecuting Shylock, who is said to possess a man's trunk but a 'currish spirit' and can therefore be treated like a mongrel dog. In *Twelfth Night*, the supposedly mad Malvolio is questioned about the same theory. 'What is the opinion of Pythagoras concerning wildfowl?' asks Feste. Malvolio staunchly upholds human supremacy, and denies that his grandmother's soul could 'haply inhabit a bird'. Rosalind in *As You Like It* is unembarrassed by her earlier lives, which unfurl backwards to 'Pythagoras' time that I was an Irish rat, which I can hardly remember'. Lance in *Two Gentlemen of Verona* puts Pythagoras to the test when he puzzles over his partnership with his scene-stealing pet dog Crab. 'I am the dog,' says Lance. 'No, the dog is himself, and I am the dog. O, the dog is me, and I am myself.' The human being feels generic, indistinguishable from 'all the kind of the Lances'; the dog, however, is more than canine, and knows how to copy human attitudes.

Shakespeare's characters are rarefied specimens, like Crab who shares and improves on the imitative talents of Isabella's 'angry ape'; whether they belong to the same species as we do is not always clear. As Oscar Wilde wondered in the preface to *The Picture of Dorian Gray*, what does Caliban see when he looks in the Shakespearean mirror?

Othello, for instance, is a conundrum. He posits a precariously high-flown notion of humanity for himself and his adored Desdemona, and enforces this when he calls the cannibals Anthropophagi: the classification makes them questionably human, because the protocols dictate that we should eat only animals we consider to be our inferiors. These hierarchical distinctions are a bequest of culture, unknown in nature. Othello even invests utensils – a napkin, a weapon – with an exotic provenance to make them worthy of belonging to him. A sibyl sewed his handkerchief from hallowed worms, and 'it was dyed in mummy, which the skillful / Conserv'd of maidens' hearts'; the sword with which he kills himself comes from Spain and is 'the ice-brook's temper'. He would rather suffer eternal perdition than admit he has been farcically duped, which is why he calls Iago a 'demi-devil', even though, after glancing at his tormenter's feet, he admits that demons with cloven hooves exist only in fables. Othello's insecure self-love collapses almost instantly into virulent self-loathing. When he begins to doubt Desdemona, he says 'Exchange me for a goat' and 'I had rather be a toad' – creatures with no conceit about their status. 'O inhuman dog!' cries Roderigo as Iago stabs him: the tautology may help him to feel better about the way he has been exploited and discarded. Timon of Athens sees through the fraud of such thinking. After his friends betray him, he adds a prefix to the Greek word for humankind and renames himself Misanthropos. Accosted by his former colleague Alcibiades, he says 'I do wish thou wert a dog, / That I might love thee something'.

The Macbeths make their own adjustments to this slithery terminology. Macbeth justifies his second thoughts about the murder of Duncan by saying 'I dare do all that may become a man'. His wife takes manhood to mean virility, and calls his hesitation unmanly; to say he is 'infirm', as she does when he refuses to return to the chamber to smear Duncan's grooms with blood, is the lowest of sexual insults. Later Macbeth tells the mercenaries whom he hires to murder Banquo that they only pass for men 'in the catalogue', just as spaniels, demi-wolves and a smattering of other breeds are designated dogs. It is a nimble-witted self-exculpation: Macbeth outsources dirty work that might be thought inhuman.

Comparing portraits, Hamlet says that his father is Hyperion, while Claudius is a satyr. His simile capriciously exalts one human being and degrades another: are we really so pliable? The two men are brothers, but in Hamlet's account one is a sun god (though in his ghostly form the dead king is a night-walker who retires underground at the first sign of russet dawn), the other a furry woodland deity (though the new king never seems so crudely phallic). Hamlet himself is at times lucidly Apollonian, while at others – when he chatters obscenely about country matters or jokes that worms are feasting on the smelly corpse of Polonius – he is perhaps not a satyr but certainly a satirist. On a level platform, Shakespeare's people soar and plummet up and down the scale of being, which for them is a Jacob's ladder made of words.

*

Nature, the goddess whose compliment Antony relays in his praise of Brutus, has no monopoly here. Ross sees Macbeth and the Thane of Cawdor, both in armour, as faceless automata,

interchangeable 'self-comparisons'. Though Macbeth is 'Bellona's bridegroom', he has no spousal or coital relationship with the goddess of war: he is simply bellicosity in male form, additionally 'lapped in proof', with extra skins of metal that make him almost robotic. Lady Macbeth malevolently remarks that 'nature's copy's not eterne' in Banquo and his son. As offprints, genetic copies not originals, they are easily replaceable and even more easily eliminated.

The Volscians venerate Coriolanus as 'a thing / Made by some other deity than Nature', and that blunt word 'thing' – which has echoes in Cordelia's obtuse 'nothing' when Lear asks for a verbal show of love, and in the blurry 'something' that Hamlet fears in the afterlife – forces us to ask all over again what kind of thing a human being is. In an explosive rant, Coriolanus says he will not allow the plebeians to fawn on his battle scars, because that means having to hear his 'nothings monster'd'. The phrase, apparently spat out impromptu, is riddled with poetic suggestion and psychological revelation. Although Coriolanus concedes that his martial aura is a nullity, made of air as words are, his meaning is far from modest. The wounds he prizes belong exclusively to him; if others even look at them, his barbed ego fears they will see him as a deformity, like the 'rarer monsters' in whose company Macduff wants to display Macbeth, or like the cockatrice – a mythical serpent with a rooster's head – that Richard III's disgusted mother says she has hatched in her womb. According to the verb that Coriolanus invents for the occasion, monstering involves a grotesque, hulking enlargement. But the word's etymology gives it another, more narcissistic implication: it allows him to be set up for demonstration, like the monstrance that shows off the consecrated Host in the Mass.

The monstrosity of Coriolanus is his fanatical uniqueness. He acts 'as if a man were author of himself / And knew no other kin', and in his egomania he threatens to 'depopulate the city and / Be

Ralph Fiennes as Coriolanus in the film that he also directed.

every man himself'. The moon-calf Caliban is a similar creation, even though his aim is not to empty a city but to fill Prospero's island with replicas of himself, which he intends to sire on Miranda. Similarly, Emilia in *Othello* calls jealousy a monster because it is a product of the brain's pullulation – artificially generated, 'begot upon itself, born on itself'. Is there an analogy with the way actors beget and bear variant selves? The Bastard in *King John* insists that 'I am I, howe'er I was begot', though when Hubert, groping in the dark, asks him who he is, he replies 'Who thou wilt.' The two phrases mark the outer limits of existential villainy or vacuity, since those who believe they have created themselves are happy to destroy others, with whom they feel no connection. Richard III boasts that he can 'frame [his] face to all occasions'. Only under duress does he retract into a unitary being, as when he fends off the ghosts of his victims and asserts his solitary occupancy of the world:

> What do I fear? Myself? There's none else by.
> Richard is Richard; that is, I am I.

Nominalism is the ego's last, desperate resort.

Iago, who has the same talent for falsifying or negating himself, says something different but means much the same when he tells Roderigo 'I am not what I am'. In *Twelfth Night* Viola utters exactly those words, with a twinge of guilt that Iago does not feel. The shared phrase is also a statement of their vocation as actors, brazenly amoral in Iago's case, morally uncomfortable in Viola's. Disguise – the very basis of theatre – is for Viola 'a wickedness'. She means that acting corrupts the plain dealing with others that makes our social existence possible. At worst, like a kind of witchcraft, it can usurp the identity of someone who is 'feelingly personated', as Maria says when she forges a love letter from Olivia to Malvolio. Ulysses in *Troilus and Cressida* slyly ridicules Agamemnon as he describes the 'o'er-wrested' performances in which Patroclus 'acts thy greatness' to amuse Achilles. Cleopatra dreads being mimicked by a boy actor with a squeaky voice, as she would have been in Shakespeare's theatre: these performers rail against vices or stylistic faults they are at the same time displaying. Hamlet criticizes actors who have neither 'th' accent of Christians nor the gait of Christian, pagan, nor man', then disregards that edict in his affected derangement. Puck specializes in the kind of exhibitionism that Hamlet pretends to dislike: he boasts of having turned himself into a roasted crab to tempt a hungry housewife or into a neighing filly to tease a randy horse – feats that he does not, alas, demonstrate onstage in *A Midsummer Night's Dream*.

Shakespeare's plays suggest that we are all artificers, amateur actors who devise one or more roles that we spend our lives performing, with society as a theatre in which we deploy an inborn talent for dissembling. Cassius in *Julius Caesar* hopes to establish his integrity when he doughtily cites 'my single self', which forbids him 'to be / In awe of such a thing as I myself' by bowing down before Caesar. He takes comfort in imagining that he is an integer; the theatre, however, entices the other selves we all contain to come out of hiding, which can be maddening. For Troilus, duality can only mean duplicity. Watching Cressida betray him by flirting with Diomedes, he bemoans his 'negation'. He first asks whether it was Cressida he saw, then says it was 'not Cressid'; unable to comprehend the change, he decides 'This is and is not Cressid'. The more of her there are, the less there is of him.

An equivalent episode occurs in *The Comedy of Errors*, with a different outcome. Antipholus of Syracuse, a stranger in Ephesus, bumps into Adriana, who is married to his twin. Though she assumes he is her husband, he denies that they know each other. She can only conclude that he is no longer himself, and worries as much about her vocabulary as his sanity. '"Thyself" I call it', she says – a psychological equivalent to the soul, but with a tendency to skip between bodies. Before long Antipholus is doting on

Luciana, Adriana's sister. She tells him to redirect his endearments to Adriana, but he insists on making love to 'thyself, mine own self's better part'. Unlike Troilus, the two women are bemused rather than distressed: people in comedy can afford to have a more supple, ductile sense of self. 'I am not as I have been', says Benedick, making light of his instant change from dislike of Beatrice to infatuation with her. After a fortuitous religious conversion, Oliver in *As You Like It* stops persecuting Orlando. ''Twas I, but 'tis not I,' he explains, and his version of the phrase places him somewhere between Iago's smugness and Viola's remorse; he is unapologetic about 'being the thing I am'.

A better option might be to rejoice in the multiplicity or complementarity of selves. Leontes and Polixenes in *The Winter's Tale* remember when they frisked like 'twinned lambs'; Leontes adds that he and his boy Mamillius are 'almost as like as eggs'. Helena and Hermia in *A Midsummer Night's Dream*, now quarrelling about their comparative height, once 'grew together / Like to a double cherry'. The twins in *Twelfth Night* resemble 'an apple, cleft in two'; when they appear together, the sundered halves are rejoined, but Antonio, mystified, asks Sebastian 'How have you made division of yourself?' His question is a searching one. What flaw in nature separated us and thereby created drama, which is a by-product of our human obsession with an individuality that sheep, eggs or pieces of fruit can do without? In *Cymbeline*, when Fidele is revived as Imogen, Arviragus says that the two are as interchangeable as grains of sand. Belarius, older and wiser, is not surprised to see 'the same dead thing alive'. 'Creatures may be alike,' he shrugs.

Antipholus first compares himself to 'a drop of water / That in the ocean seeks another drop', which he assumes is impossible; Adriana later warns him that he cannot 'fall / A drop of water in the breaking gulf, / And take unmingled thence that drop again'. The play proves them wrong. Adriana thinks that she and her husband should be 'undividable, incorporate', and so they are in this liquid continuum, which – thanks to the sea's tidal separation and reunion of Egeon's family – resembles Freud's 'oceanic feeling', the sense of complementary, limitless being we are said to lose after infancy. Put through the farcical action of the play, its characters abandon the notion that people should have an outline or boundary, a defence against merging with others or being immersed in everything; they are at first confused and then delighted by errors about identity that are actually a dissolution of identity. Antony, preparing to die after his defeat at Actium, arrives at a similar self-reappraisal. He studies a moist, mutating cloud that successively resembles a bear, a lion or a citadel and, as he says, 'mock[s] our eyes with air'. 'Here I am Antony,' he tells Eros, 'yet cannot hold this visible shape.' Death will be simply one more change in a physical state that is molten, never constant.

Some Shakespearean characters are eager for what Don Pedro in *Much Ado About Nothing* calls trans-shaping, or even for a kind of transubstantiation. 'Are you a god? would you create me new?' Antipholus asks Luciana. 'Transform me then,' he begs. Coriolanus remembers a time when Menenius 'godded me, indeed'. The linguistic daring of the phrase is equalled by its intellectual audacity: it is a shock to hear that noun used as a verb, especially a transitive one. A god usually occupies a fixed, still point, like the northern star to which Caesar likens himself; the verb makes godhead a mark of favour bestowed from below – another example of the way that Shakespeare's theatre redesigns the world. In electing gods, as Caliban does by worshipping the sottish Stephano, we bow down before unworthy idols. When Pompey in *Antony and Cleopatra* addresses the triumvirs as 'senators alone of this great world, / Chief factors for the gods', his words have a needling acuity: senators are politicians, and the opportunistic alliance of Antony, Octavius and Lepidus soon falters. Iachimo in *Cymbeline* describes Posthumus as 'a descended god', though he sours the compliment by also calling him 'a holy witch', which attributes his attractiveness to occult powers. Desdemona sadly tells Emilia 'we must think men are not gods'.

In the history plays Shakespeare capsizes a hierarchy that is political rather than religious, and he does so simply by twisting an honorific noun and an adjective into verbs. Richard II reflects that kings can only 'monarchize' for as long as the ceremonial imposture lasts, and Richard III remembers how he schemed to 'royalize' his clan by conspiring against their rivals. If a character can be godded, he can easily be kinged or, to use Richard II's self-pitying word, 'unkinged'. A value that was absolute, supposedly sustained by divine favour, crumbles or is sub-divided: in *King John* the dying ruler says he is now no more than 'a clod, / And module of confounded royalty'. Language is modular, and many-syllabled words can be broken down into clods, grains, specks of dust; the Latin root of John's word 'module' goes to work almost virally to remind us that everything is always modulating, changing and decaying, becoming outmoded. Cade in *Henry VI* jeers at the titular gradations upheld by language when he kneels to knight himself. Equally impudent, Joan of Arc announces that 'God's mother deignèd to appear to me' and 'infused on me / That beauty am I bless'd with which you see'. Vanity is her divine right.

People in the comedies despair of humanity, or worry about what connection they can have with creatures who, tailor-made like Oswald, are masked and mannered confections. Besieged by fortune-hunters from England, Scotland, Germany, Naples and Morocco, Portia in *The Merchant of Venice* has lost faith in the humanist notion of a divine prototype from which we all supposedly derive. 'God made him,' she says of her French suitor, 'and therefore let him pass for a man': the remark suggests that she has little respect for God's skill or discernment. Olivia in *Twelfth Night* is more curious about the human genus and its quaint variants. 'What kind o' man is he?' she enquires when informed that Cesario wishes to speak to her. 'Why, of mankind', says Malvolio, affecting indifference. His sniffy vagueness is apt, because the androgynous page belongs to *homo sapiens* but happens not to be male. Malvolio's compound term is no guarantee of fellow-feeling, and it is employed accusingly by the tribune in *Coriolanus* when Volumnia harangues him. 'Are you mankind?' he asks: kindness is a component of the word, and it holds us to a biological compact that ought to make us akin. Volumnia, however, refuses to belong to the same species as Sicinius, and she retaliates by accusing him of 'foxship'. At its crudest, identification involves a lewd physical inspection. Pandarus, pimping for Troilus, asks Cressida 'Do you know a man if you see him?'

In other contexts the enquiry is agitated by the suspicion that man may not be the measure of all things. Banquo carefully interrogates the witches, first demanding 'Live you?', then wanting to know 'are you aught / That man may question?' A Renaissance man like Hamlet, at the centre of a world arranged around him, could question everything and expect a reasonable answer; that confidence eludes Banquo. More playfully open-minded characters know that such categories are permeable. 'A man or a fish?' muses Trinculo when he stumbles over Caliban. 'O flesh, flesh, how art thou fishified!' exclaims Mercutio as Romeo returns from a supposed night of love: his upstanding manliness may have turned limp and wriggly following contact with a woman.

The most protracted of these inquisitions comes when Pericles is reunited with his lost daughter Marina. Incredulous, he wonders

> are you flesh and blood?
> Have you a working pulse and are no fairy?
> Motion as well? Speak on. Where were you born,
> And wherefore call'd Marina?

The interrogation first suggests the clinical watchfulness of the doctor who observes Lady Macbeth as she sleepwalks, yet at the same time Pericles is as stupefied as Banquo when he asks the witches 'Are ye fantastical?' or as mistrustful as Evans in *The Merry Wives of Windsor* who, in a forest over-run by sprites and goblins, says 'I smell a man of middle earth'. Pericles' initial queries are scientific, taxonomic, like Shakespeare's question to the supernaturally beautiful loved one in the fifty-third sonnet: 'What is your substance, whereof are you made?' It may seem odd that Pericles should ask about motion, and in many texts this query is instead printed as an exclamation. Hamlet, however, specifies that man 'in form and moving' is 'express and admirable': we are kinetically designed, capable of express speed if pressure is applied. Wanting to be reassured, Pericles acknowledges that we qualify as animals because we are animate – an advantage in the short term, although it dooms us to a shorter life than that enjoyed by vegetables and minerals, or by the dead Lucy in Wordsworth's 'A Slumber Did My Spirit Seal', who has 'no motion' and 'no force' yet is still 'Rolled round in earth's diurnal course / With rocks, and stones, and trees'. Pericles finally closes in on personal identification, adding two queries about provenance and nomenclature. When Marina announces that she was 'born at sea', the etymology authenticates her.

After all this abstruse quibbling about who or what human beings are, the problem is restated in plainspoken prose. Fraternizing incognito with his soldiers on the night before the battle, Henry V says 'the King is but a man, as I am... His ceremonies laid by, in his nakedness he appears but a man'. The absence of clothes herds us together; we are equalized as what Falstaff, describing his raggle-taggle conscripts in *Henry IV*, calls 'mortal men, mortal men', destined to be consumed by the earth or dispersed in the air like smoke. 'Well, we are all mortal,' says Beatrice in *Much Ado About Nothing* after deriding Benedick as a stuffed toy. Cloten in *Cymbeline* sarcastically exclaims 'What mortality is!' a few minutes before he is negligently slaughtered offstage. Although the drunkard Barnadine in *Measure for Measure* is 'insensible of mortality', he remains 'desperately mortal', refusing to die – like Desdemona as she negotiates with Othello – to serve the plot's convenience. Humanity is what we aspire to possess; about mortality we have no choice.

Torn between exposure and concealment, the two opposed imperatives of drama, Shakespeare's people engage in a bewildered or agonized quest for understanding. Self-consciousness replaces scrutiny by Calderón's Author, but self-knowledge is hard to attain. We see ourselves only by reflection, as Cassius tells Brutus when offering to be his looking glass and to 'modestly discover to yourself / That of yourself which you yet know not of'. Achilles presses the same point in *Troilus and Cressida*: the eye seeks validation from someone else's eye, and

> speculation turns not to itself
> Till it hath travell'd, and is mirror'd there
> Where it may see itself.

But the vantage point remains frontal, superficial, incapable of insight because it craves reciprocation. Menenius in *Coriolanus* calls for something more exacting and more awkward when he tells the tribunes that he wishes they 'could turn your eyes toward the napes of your necks, and make but an interior survey of your good selves!' Regardless of our contortions, this is the view that Shakespeare's theatre recommends.

Scene Individable,
Or Poem Unlimited

Tedious brief
Tragical-comical
Historical-pastoral
Seasons and genres
Killing and dying
Mapping a microcosm

With a fond, jocular sense of comradeship, Shakespeare allowed two sets of colleagues to define the unruly plays he wrote. At Elsinore and in Athens, those troupes flaunt bills of fare that are inimitably Shakespearean. The players in *Hamlet* cater to all tastes with their 'tragical-comical-historical-pastoral' hodgepodge. The rude mechanicals in *A Midsummer Night's Dream* rely on paradox or oxymoron rather than that hyphenated hybrid: what they offer is 'very tragical mirth', and Theseus chooses their bumbling farce about Pyramus and Thisbe over other more learned submissions on subjects that include the crazed Dionysian women tearing Orpheus limb from limb – an episode that Nietzsche associated with the birth of tragedy in Greece.

The players who visit Elsinore announce that 'Seneca cannot be too heavy, nor Plautus too light' for them. Shakespeare took Seneca and Plautus as models early in his career: *Titus Andronicus*, in which Tamora eats a pie that contains the minced bodies of her sons, has a precedent in Seneca's *Thyestes*, and *The Comedy of Errors* closely follows the *Menaechmi* of Plautus, about identical twins who are mistaken for each another. But Shakespeare typically edges tragic solemnity and comic levity closer together. The horrors of *Titus Andronicus* open into a grotesquely pantheistic account of carnivorous nature and the comic gluttony with which it feasts on us; in *The Comedy of Errors*, jest tips over into earnest as characters reel through a potentially deadly delirium which is, as Egeon says, their 'night of life'.

The company in *Hamlet* also advertises a 'scene individable, or poem unlimited'. Divisions and limits were strictly enforced in classical drama, where the action was confined to a single day in a single place. Shakespeare evades the unities of time and place, even when technically abiding by them in *The Comedy of Errors* and *The Tempest*. In Ephesus and on Prospero's island, the happenings of a few hours recapitulate the events of the previous two decades, bringing back together people who are the flotsam and jetsam of a wider maritime world. Later plays abandon any pretence of concision. *Pericles*, set 'dispersedly in various countries', wanders around the eastern Mediterranean; *Antony and Cleopatra* alternates between Alexandria and Rome, with an unstageable naval battle in the Ionian Sea as its turning point.

Shakespeare's poetic drama is unlimited because it is always partly in prose. At Caesar's funeral, Brutus begs his countrymen to 'hear me for my cause, and be silent that you may hear me'. Antony then asks the same audience to 'lend me your ears', which, behind the extravagant politeness of the periphrasis, is more intimate and ingratiating than Brutus's call to order. Brutus makes his case in temperate prose, and the listeners calmly assent; Antony's versified oration ignites a riot. In *Othello*, by contrast, the poetic fustian of a hero who calls his mental powers 'my speculative and officed instruments' is brought low by Iago's colloquial wit, and by Emilia's brutally prosaic charge that he is 'as ignorant as dirt!'

Bottom and his workmates garble the classical opposites by promising a 'Lamentable Comedy' that will be 'tedious brief'. Tedium is not a problem in Shakespeare: as the Chorus says in *Henry V*, a play is an hour-glass. Tragedy has an imperative haste, synchronized with the impatience of Macbeth riding 'sharp as his spur' or Lady Macbeth discerning 'the future in the instant'. But the meanderings of narrators with long memories slow down this rush, and give the drama a dual tempo. Polonius is prolix, the Nurse rambles on about weaning Juliet, and Mistress Quickly relates in digressive detail the events of the 'Wednesday in Wheeson week' when Falstaff proposed to her. 'Wit,' as Iago explains to Cassio, 'depends on dilatory time', and comedy also permits people to enjoy the succession of tomorrows that Macbeth has no interest in living through. When Touchstone marries Audrey in *As You Like It*, Jaques jokes that 'thy loving voyage / Is but for two months victuall'd': a cynical prediction, but he still assumes that they will outlast the play. Hence too Desdemona's negotiation with Othello when she pleads 'Kill me tomorrow; let me live tonight!' Another day – even if unhappy, as it certainly would have been – is worth bargaining for.

Whether their lives are comic or tragic, preserved by what Falstaff calls 'the saltness of time' or else summarily cut short, Shakespeare's characters are always historical. In *Twelfth Night*, a priest is brought on to testify that he has married Olivia and Sebastian. In several ceremonious lines he expatiates on their 'contract of eternal bond of love', after which he steps back from blissful eternity into mortal time and lonely celibacy: since the wedding, he says, 'my watch hath told me, toward my grave / I have travell'd but two hours'. This one wistful, generous, fussily verbose speech ensures that we will never forget him. A time-check at the end of *King Lear* is more chilling. Edgar says that he made himself known to his father 'some half-hour past'. In performance this happened only minutes before, so the detail alerts us to the play's hurtling abbreviation of life.

Characters in the history plays are oppressed by their own temporality. The conspiratorial Archbishop in *Henry IV* adjudicates between tenses, remarking that 'Past and to come seem best; things present worst.' He prefers the dead past or the unborn future because to live in the moment, as actors also do, is to confront our existential flimsiness, our constant need to decide on a next move that may be our last. Hastings dolefully replies 'We are time's subjects, and time bids be gone.' History is a killer, impatient to dispense with these tenuous, anxious men by consigning them to its written record of defeat and failure.

Richard II begins with the king addressing his uncle as 'time-honoured Gaunt'; his own authority is threatened when Northumberland omits such flummery and refers to him as 'Richard', before defensively explaining 'Only to be brief / Left I his title out'. While Richard retains power, he can use it to pass sentences that comprise extended stretches of time. He exiles

Bolingbroke for a decade, then on a whim reduces the term to six years. 'How long a time lies in one little word!' says Bolingbroke, amazed that 'the breath of kings' can remit 'four lagging winters and four wanton springs'. Crowned as Henry IV, he finds that he is acting out a predetermined history. He remorsefully recalls a speech in which Richard foretold 'this same time's condition', and goes on to ask 'Are these things then necessities?' Prince Hal, less constrained, wastes time with Falstaff, who is indifferent to temporal directives. Questioned about his age by the Lord Chief Justice, Falstaff names the time of day he was born but not the year, and says that he had the same round belly when he was an infant. Hal, however, thinks ahead to 'redeeming time' as he plots his reformation. In a game, he rehearses his banishment of Falstaff, who assumes that everything in the theatre is pretence or playful hypothesis, and bluffly begs to be spared. Hal repeats the verdict as if it were already immutably written into history. 'I do', he says; then, advancing to a retributive future tense, he vows 'I will'.

Shaken by the hazards of war and politics, historical characters are fatalists. 'O gentlemen, the time of life is short', exclaims Hotspur, refusing to peruse letters that are probably already out of date. Life, he says, rides 'upon a dial's point, / Still ending at the arrival of an hour'. Brevity impels these people to operate at speed, twisting, veering and manoeuvring as they go. Richard III makes the headlong race more interesting by placing obstacles in his own way for the sheer pleasure of vaulting over them. Wooing Lady Anne, he admits that he killed her husband and her father-in-law; offered the crown he has murdered to attain, he at first tells his supporters 'I cannot, nor I will not, yield to you'. Reckless and anarchically impulsive, he sabotages the sense of predictability that we hope to derive from history. In one short scene, at a meeting convened to arrange the coronation of his nephew, he arrives late, apologizes for over-sleeping, then avoids discussion of what Buckingham calls 'the royal time' by idly asking a bishop to send for some strawberries from his garden, after which he briefly withdraws. He returns in a factitious fury to round on a man who was an ally moments ago and accuse him of treachery. 'Off with his head', he snaps, swearing 'I will not dine until I see the same.' He then storms out, perhaps to eat the strawberries.

The antidote to such flurries of plotting is pastoral, the last and most placidly undramatic of the genres that the Elsinore players conflate. Here time ploddingly follows agricultural routine, as in the shepherd's life that Henry VI longs for:

> So minutes, hours, days, weeks, months, and years
> Past over to the end they were created,
> Would bring white hairs unto a quiet grave.

Although Clarence in *Henry IV* derides 'the old folk, / Time's doting chronicles', he ought to envy them: they chronicle the seasons, the crops, the weather, all of which are comfortingly repetitive, not the political upsets recorded by historians. On a farm in Gloucestershire, Shallow's servant Davy asks 'Shall we sow the headland with wheat?' and reminds his master that a bucket needs repairing. Shallow questions his cousin Silence about the price of bullocks at Stamford fair; Silence cannot say, not having been there, though it is likely that Shallow already knew that, or was not surprised to be hear it – this is how old acquaintances talk, not exchanging information but helping time to pass, as Shallow does when he says 'Certain, 'tis certain; very sure, very sure'. What reassures him, and gives the utterance its nodding, contented rhythm, is the certainty of death, since he and Silence are discussing friends who have preceded them into the ground. In this unmapped outpost, there is a sudden, piercing recognition of a world elsewhere. After listening to Shallow reminisce about his frolics in the city more than fifty years before, Davy quietly says 'I hope to see London once ere I die.' Presumably he didn't.

The most reliable chronometer is the body. Cleopatra's remark that she is 'wrinkled deep in time' is not a complaint about ageing; those wrinkles comfortably embed her in her flesh, and commemorate the laughter that produced them. When Falstaff asks the time of day, Hal calls the request 'superfluous' because his only appointments are mealtime and bedtime, which punctually announce themselves in his belly and his drowsy head. Rosalind asks Orlando the same question, and he replies 'There's no clock in the forest.' True, we ripen and rot – as Jaques puts it when enumerating the ages of man – without being told to do so by a clock, or even by Falstaff's chimes at midnight. Rosalind, however, understands the relativity of Shakespearean time, which is both tedious and brief, a laggard and a wielder of what Milton in his pastoral elegy 'Lycidas' calls 'th' abhorred shears'. As she explains to Orlando, time 'travels in divers paces with divers persons', variously ambling, trotting, galloping as well as standing still – and in *As You Like It* we watch events at all those tempi.

When Orlando arrives an hour late, Rosalind chides him by pointing out that someone in love is liable to 'divide a minute into a thousand parts' and fret about the decelerated seconds: she might be thinking of Juliet, who agrees to send a message to Romeo at nine the next morning and immediately afterwards complains that it is twenty years till then. Rosalind takes a longer view, and when Orlando threatens to die for love she reminds him that 'The poor world is almost six thousand years old', which means that everything that could happen has already happened, and after a quick survey of the historical evidence she concludes that there is no precedent for dying 'in a love cause'. In this pastoral play – which begins with Orlando saying 'As I remember, Adam', as if he could recollect Eden – that glance backwards at the earth's immemorial age quietly subverts Shakespeare's own form: our crises are not unique or new, so why should we over-dramatize them?

The Elsinore playbill begins by splicing together tragedy and comedy. According to classical theory, the two dramatic forms took such different views of human nature that they were mutually exclusive. A choice between opposed absolutes was required, an act of philosophical partisanship: dramatists could deal with people who either were noble but flawed, or with those who were base and contemptible. Neoclassicists made this disparity a matter of social class. Voltaire said that tragedy should be about the ambition of princes, whereas comedy examined the petty, mercenary cravings of the bourgeoisie.

Shakespeare's plays recognize no such division. In them, tragedy and comedy intertwine, merge, collide and change places. 'At the same time', as Samuel Johnson said in the preface to his edition, 'the reveller is hastening to his wine, and the mourner burying his friend'. Comic beginnings and tragic endings repeatedly overlap. Theseus, preparing to marry in *A Midsummer Night's Dream*, wants to 'turn melancholy forth to funerals', only to be waylaid by Egeus, who threatens his refractory daughter Hermia with death. *The Comedy of Errors* likewise begins with Egeon's morose acceptance of a legal verdict that will 'by the doom of death end woes and all'. In *As You Like It* the Duke banishes Rosalind and threatens that if she delays 'you die'. In *Twelfth Night* Viola and Olivia are both mourning recently deceased brothers, and *All's Well That Ends Well* opens with the widowed Countess telling her son Bertram that when he departs 'I bury a second husband'.

Capulet orders a hymeneal festival turned to 'black funeral' after Juliet is discovered comatose. A funeral and a wedding coincide uneasily at the start of *Hamlet*; later, Ophelia's bier – as Gertrude says while throwing flowers in her grave – is a substitute for her bridal bed. The opposites violently fuse when Richard III's mother curses her womb as 'the bed of death'; a grislier and more repellent conjunction occurs when Richard persuades his sister-in-law to pimp for him with his niece. He nonchalantly admits that he killed her sons,

> But in your daughter's womb I bury them,
> Where, in that nest of spicery, they will breed
> Selves of themselves, to your recomforture.

The 'joy, pleasance, revel' that celebrate Othello's nuptials are the cause of Cassio's degradation. And is the spoilsport who suppresses the party a comic ogre or a tragic malefactor? When Malvolio chides Sir Toby, he says 'ye make an alehouse of my lady's house'; Goneril, castigating Lear's knights, claims that they have turned her court into 'a riotous inn', 'a tavern or a brothel'. The ban leads in one case to a malicious practical joke, in the other to an infanticidal curse and a rush towards self-destruction.

Shakespearean comedy can be as lethal as tragedy. 'If you tickle us,' demands Shylock in his accusation of the Christians, 'do we not laugh?' That mirthless hilarity registers discomfort or outright distress: as Hero says in *Much Ado About Nothing*, we can 'die with tickling'. Beatrice begins by archly inquiring about the tally of Moors slain in battle by Benedick, but when she later challenges him to 'Kill Claudio' she is not joking. 'He kills her in her own humour', says Peter in *The Taming of the Shrew* as he watches Petruchio starve and bully Kate. Aaron in *Titus Andronicus* boasts of having dug up corpses and seated them on the doorsteps of their former friends as a prank. Enjoying such atrocities, he says he 'almost broke my heart with extreme laughter'. Puck has the same reaction to the 'jangling' of the mortals he drives to despair. The same extremity approaches again when Iago jeers at the epileptic Othello, when the Fool ridicules the humbled Lear, and when Feste mocks Malvolio in the dark room. Such laughter is as contagious as a mob's hysteria, and it should probably hurt, to punish us for our cruelty. Aristotle denied that the grimacing comic mask registered genuine pain; Shakespeare offers no such reassurance.

In *Love's Labour's Lost* amorous frolics and verbal froth are curtailed by the sudden announcement that the Princess's father is dead. Berowne is sent to jest in a hospital, to test whether mirth can 'move a soul in agony'. The experiment will last for a year: 'too long for a play,' he says – ejected from comedy, he also reaches the limits of drama, which demands closure. As the characters disperse, a song of floral spring is followed by another that describes punitive winter, with red chafed noses, milk frozen in the pail, and birds brooding on skeletal boughs. The genres follow each other as inevitably as the seasons, bent into an eternal circle.

Comedy and tragedy both have pastoral roots, corresponding to the quarrel between sap-filled youth and crabby age in one of Shakespeare's sonnets from *The Passionate Pilgrim*:

> Youth like summer morn, age like winter weather;
> Youth like summer brave, age like winter bare.

The ardent Fenton in *The Merry Wives of Windsor* 'speaks holiday' and 'smells April and May', though when Pandarus says that Troilus weeps for Cressida 'like a man born in April', she scoffs at those showers by replying 'I'll spring up in his tears an't were a nettle against May'. Richard III applies the seasonal metaphor to regime change. Discontented winter has given way to balmy summer with his brother's accession to the throne, and he asks the 'fair sun' to 'shine out, till I have bought a glass' in which he can admire his own crooked shadow. But in speeding up the cycle he brings death nearer, for others if not himself. Hearing his young nephew make precocious plans for his eventual reign, Richard snarls 'Short summers lightly have a forward spring'; soon the boy is murdered in the Tower. Cleopatra, imagining herself to be vegetation, jokes about her 'salad days, / When I was green in judgement', and Enobarbus expects her never to wither or grow stale. But Macbeth feels himself lapsing into 'the sere, the yellow leaf', just as Shakespeare's seventy-third sonnet says that fading autumn is the 'time of year thou mayst in me behold'. 'A sad tale's best for winter', as Mamillius tells Hermione when deciding what kind of story to tell her. He chooses well, since they both soon die. Spring resurrects the dead Hermione, though the season of growth is delayed for sixteen years, and the resurgent comedy cannot bring back Mamillius.

The sequence that leads from wintry tragedy to vernal comedy can also be jarred awry. 'The seasons alter', Titania says in *A Midsummer Night's Dream*: her feud with Oberon angers the moon, causes 'distemperature', and muddles the landscape's 'wonted liveries', so that hoar frosts blight the roses, and trees that ought to be bare wear a mocking coronet of summer buds. When Puck drives the lovers out of comedy and into potential tragedy, we watch a dizzy cycle that is diurnal rather than annual. Oberon's sorcery is his 'night-rule', and Puck prevails until all 'damnèd spirits' retire to 'their wormy beds' at dawn. Daylight, however, does not banish such ghouls. Gertrude is dismayed by Hamlet's 'nighted colour', and the widowed queen in *Richard III* expects to follow Edward IV 'to his new kingdom of ne'er-changing night': like Proserpine she will descend to the realm of Pluto, though without being granted a seasonal reprieve when spring revives the earth.

Downcast characters in *King Lear* take comfort from the likelihood that tragedy will sooner or later relax into comedy. Pinioned in the stocks, Kent stoically waits for morning: 'Fortune, good night; smile once more; turn thy wheel.' Edgar welcomes his destitution on the heath, because 'The worst returns to laughter' – though then, encountering his blinded father, he realizes that the wheel has reversed again: 'Who is 't can say "I am at the worst"? / I am worse than e'er I was.' Edgar and Hamlet share a proverbial wisdom about how we should live and die. Hamlet says that 'The readiness is all', and Edgar – who sweetens the tag to suggest that pain seasons us or brings us to maturity – tells Gloucester that 'Ripeness is all'. The boatswain in *The Tempest* has gruffer advice for his passengers, who panic when they think they are about to drown. 'Give thanks you have lived so long,' he says, 'and make yourselves ready.' The conceit of tragedy is its pretence that, as Hector says in *Troilus and Cressida*, 'the end crowns all'. In Shakespeare's plays, lives are more likely to end abruptly, broken off without warning and with no chance for famous last words.

*

Death is inevitable but tragedy is optional, and in Shakespeare it is usually avoidable. Romeo does not receive the message about Juliet's sham death; he poisons himself in despair, and she regains consciousness just as he needlessly dies. 'Great thing of us forgot!' cries Albany, who has left Lear and Cordelia in peril. This involuntary or accidental timing goes against the wilfulness of tragic characters, who are determined to exit on their own terms: the Antigone of Sophocles hangs herself because she does not recognize the state's right to execute her, and Lavinia in Eugene O'Neill's *Mourning Becomes Electra* chooses immurement in her funereal house.

Warned of danger by auguries and by his wife's nightmare, Caesar coolly points out that death is 'a necessary end', a biological cessation, and reasons that it 'will come when it will come' – but when it does come he forgets such resignation and dies with an eye on the historical record. He first quotes a Latin reproach to Brutus taken from later chronicles, and only after that consents to collapse: 'Then fall Caesar', he says, directing his performance. Such studied Roman gestures, like the 'voluntary wound' Portia gives herself to convince Brutus of her valour, express an aristocratic contempt for life – classically seemly, yet bloodless and emotionally stultified. Brutus informs Cassius that Portia has swallowed fire, although when Messala later mentions her death he pretends not to know about it and shrugs off his loss: 'Why, farewell, Portia. We must die, Messala.' His self-control has a uniquely Shakespearean ambivalence: is it vanity, preoccupation, or does it hint at the individual's self-suppression in a society that denies people private lives and assesses them as public things, which is what the word 'republic' means?

Given the chance, Shakespeare's tragic characters would prefer the comic continuation of their lives. Hamlet theorizes about suicide, but has no intention of going through with it; absorbed by his plots and his play-acting, he is enjoying himself too much. Lear hopes to outlast all worldly 'great ones', happily imprisoned with Cordelia. Richard III batters a messenger who brings bad news, so desperate is he to keep tragedy at bay. Unlike Lady Macbeth welcoming the hoarse, baleful croak of the raven, Richard cries 'Out on ye, owls! Nothing but songs of death.' Macbeth too hopes 'to be safely thus', secure on the throne and protected by the witches' charm, and he mixes physical effort with metaphysics in the hope of outrunning time and escaping consequences. As he muses on the prophecies, he refers to 'this bank and shoal of time' – the shallows of the present, where we ignorantly paddle – and wishes he could 'jump the life to come', escaping judgement with a leap across the river. At one point he does hypocritically wish for death. 'Had I but died an hour before this chance,' he says after Duncan's murder is discovered, 'I had lived a blessed time'. It is a moment of supreme effrontery: as he confesses during his trip to the witches' lair, he actually expects to 'live the lease of nature, pay his breath / To time and mortal custom'. Feeble the woman's tailor in *Henry IV* agrees to be conscripted because, as he puts it in an echo of Caesar, 'A man can die but once. We owe God a death.' Macbeth's comment – with its legalistic phrasing, its references to lease and custom or to breathing as a debt – reveals his assumption that nature and time owe him a life, and a long one.

Only Othello embraces tragedy, almost making love to it. Reunited with Desdemona in Cyprus, he says 'If it were now to die / 'Twere now to be most happy' and, unlike Macbeth wishing he had predeceased Duncan, he means it. Desdemona recoils from the idea of a blissful, instantaneous death, and touches wood:

> The heavens forbid
> But that our loves and comforts should increase,
> Even as our days do grow.

As he prepares to kill himself, Othello looks forward to what he calls 'my journey's end', which he further aggrandizes into the 'very sea-mark of my utmost sail'. Tragedy, when not written by Shakespeare, confers an unwonted value on such vainglorious deaths. Henrik Ibsen's architect in *The Master Builder* plummets from a church steeple, and Hedda Gabler blows her brains out with a duelling pistol, which prompts Judge Brack to remark in amazement 'People don't do such things' – a compliment to her fanatical contempt for living happily ever after. Othello, by contrast, was never in command of the voyage or able to decide on the destination, and despite the story he tells about slaying a Turk who slandered Venice, there is no equivalence between that act of partisan policing and the easy way out he takes when he stabs himself.

Shakespearean actors sometimes choose to die spectacularly – in a Stratford production in 1959, Laurence Olivier's Coriolanus hung suspended upside down from a high platform after being stabbed by Aufidius; Toshiro Mifune, the samurai Macbeth in Akira Kurosawa's film *Throne of Blood*, ends pierced by dozens of arrows, one of which enters his neck and skewers his throat from side to side as he staggers downstairs grunting in protest – but the

Olivier as the dead Coriolanus and Anthony Nicholls
as Aufidius at Stratford in 1959.

plays do nothing to encourage such mad bravado. Antony, informed of Cleopatra's suicide, asks his attendant Eros to kill him. Eros adroitly slays himself instead; Antony has to manage without an accomplice, and falls on his sword at the wrong angle. Wounded but not dead, he implores the guards to finish him off. They refuse, and instead eulogize the great man whose behaviour is anything but heroic. His ultimate gesture turns out to have been unnecessary, as he realizes when Diomed tells him that Cleopatra has sent a false report of her death to make him feel guilty. 'Too late', says Antony: here is another Shakespearean tragedy of errors. He is then cumbrously hauled up into Cleopatra's monument, where she grieves and rails while he, unheeded, begs for a sip of wine and the chance to 'speak a little'. These mishaps are rewritten into conformity with Roman tragic etiquette when the news is passed on to Octavius, who wonders why a commemorative earthquake has not 'shook lions into civil streets'. Dercetas, bringing with him Antony's sword, offers a stilted and inaccurate account of a scene he did not witness:

> that self hand
> Which writ his honour in the acts it did,
> Hath, with the courage which the heart did lend it,
> Splitted the heart.

Cleopatra, having watched Antony's pitiful agony, contrives a smoother exit for herself. Endearingly unstoical, she researches 'easy ways to die', and wants to be sure that the asp's bite will afford pleasure not pain.

Shakespeare demolishes the notion of death as the prerogative of those who possess what A. C. Bradley called 'spiritual value' and who do not suffer from pusillanimous physical qualms. Instead, with grisly exactitude, the plays follow the physiological anguish of dying. The ghost in *Hamlet* testifies posthumously, describing how the poison that Claudius poured into the 'porches' of his ears coursed like quicksilver through the 'gates and alleys' of his body. With those images he turns himself into an invaded city; then, using metaphors that are culinary as well as medical, he reports on an organic change that curdled his 'thin and wholesome blood' and 'like eager droppings into milk' thickened it into the consistency of a posset. The tincture's eagerness is especially chilling: 'eager' means sour or pungent as well as keen, so the word simultaneously gives the henbane a taste or smell and suggests that the plant's juice takes a positive delight in its deadliness. His skin, he goes on, was encrusted, scaled or 'barked': he has experienced the kind of metamorphosis that in Ovid's fables turns a nymph into a tree, though fancy is here replaced by torment.

Other characters relate terrifying premonitions about this transitional rite. Minutes before he is shoved head-first into a wine butt, Clarence in *Richard III* relives a nightmare in which he drowns, with 'dreadful noise of waters' in his ears and visions of men gnawed by slimy fish. Claudio in *Measure for Measure* advances further into bleak non-existence:

> Ay, but to die, and go we know not where;
> To lie in cold obstruction, and to rot;
> This sensible warm motion to become
> A kneaded clod...

– and so he continues, unbearably imagining the torture of a body that ought to be insentient. Poetry is his purgatory, conveying how it might feel to be frozen in 'thick-ribbed ice' or 'blown with restless violence round about / The pendent world' by howling gales. An imagination like this, as Victor Hugo said of Shakespeare, is an uncomfortable or alarming thing to possess – an enemy inside your head that devises daylight nightmares and then preserves them in words whose lyrical beauty renders them indelible.

Matters are even more snarled when the plays deal with killing rather than dying. Hegel's philosophy made tragedy responsible for testing and strengthening moral order, which in Shakespeare's plays is hard to reconcile with the messy business of taking a life. Brutus and his fellow assassins plan to be 'sacrificers but not butchers' or 'purgers, not murderers'. Aristotle's theory of tragic catharsis promised a medicinal purgation of the body politic; Portia shares this belief in the remedy, and chides Brutus for risking his health in 'the rheumy and unpurgèd air' of the dank morning. But although the conspirators hope to 'carve [Caesar] as a dish fit for the gods, / Not hew him as a carcass fit for hounds', the difference between carving and hewing – a dish set on an altar as against offal thrown to dogs – is merely verbal. When Desdemona resists, Othello upbraids her for making 'what I intend to do / A murder, which I thought a sacrifice!' The sacrificial beast, in his view, should feel honoured to take part in the ritual. Othello disdains both carving and hewing, and chooses to execute Desdemona bloodlessly by smothering her. His priestly protocols, however, do not cancel out the savagery of his earlier vow to 'chop her into messes!'

'Kill, kill, kill, kill, kill, kill!' cries Lear, imagining a massacre that is indiscriminate but luckily hypothetical. More to the point, the rabid Hector tells Achilles 'I'll kill thee everywhere, yea, o'er and o'er', and Cade in *Henry VI* threatens to have Lord Saye beheaded ten times. They might be raving or joking, but they would prefer not to be. We die once only, as Caesar and Feeble agree; psychopaths like Aaron or Richard III chafe at that limitation, because killing allows them to participate in what Gloucester in *King Lear* calls the sport of the gods, who amuse themselves by smiting men as if swatting flies. Bradley, explicating Hegel's aesthetics, said that tragedy concerned the 'intestinal warfare of the ethical substance'. In Shakespeare, the intestines are not so conceptual. 'I'll lug the guts into the neighbour room' says Hamlet, unethically disposing of Polonius's body.

Rosencrantz orates about 'the cease of majesty', and Guildenstern alludes to the 'holy and religious fear' that tragedy in theory should induce. But they do so to fawn on Claudius, who in the event ceases unmajestically, whimpering 'O yet defend me, friends; I am but hurt' when Hamlet stabs him. Long before that final undignified cry, Claudius calmly observes that 'All that lives must die' and asks Hamlet why his father's death seems 'so particular with thee' – a shrewdly worded query, because Hamlet wants to be a particle, an exception to the rule, refusing to see himself as part of some more general whole. Shallow in *Henry IV* quotes the Psalmist and reminds Falstaff that 'All must die'. That applies to Henry IV himself: Warwick's obituary begins by announcing 'He's walked the way of nature'.

The self-importance of tragic characters is rebuked whenever the death of a non-human creature is mentioned – which, in plays grounded in pastoral, happens frequently. Jaques in *As You Like It* grieves over the death of the stag, although only because it serves his purpose as a satirist: he derides a passing herd, 'fat and greasy citizens', for not commiserating with the stricken beast. Are animals at fault because they are unsentimental? Thersites in *Troilus and Cressida* also misses the point when he sneers at waterflies, those 'diminutives of nature'. Nature does have a pecking order, but species are ranked by size and killing power rather than being differentiated by a moral scheme. When Marcus kills a fly, Titus Andronicus praises its 'pretty buzzing' and filmy wings, and pities its bereaved family. Marcus then tells him that the fly was black, like Aaron; Titus furiously wishes he could kill it again. The episode warns against our selfish folly in making more defenceless creatures take the blame for our afflictions. Hamlet's view of man's primacy among the animals can be challenged, because the beings we look down on – good to be eaten, or else expunged as vermin – have an ignorance we should envy: they do not take death as a personal affront, or spend their little lives protesting against its injustice.

Isabella in *Measure for Measure* challenges tragedy's unequal apportioning of pain and its grading of deaths when she claims that

> the poor beetle, that we tread upon,
> In corporal sufferance finds a pang as great
> As when a giant dies.

She makes the case to persuade Claudio to save her from the pang of being ravished by Angelo, though she leaves us to decide whether she is closer to the insect or the ogre. Wounded in a sword fight, Mercutio in *Romeo and Juliet* regards his fate with plucky detachment: 'Zounds, a dog, a rat, a mouse, a cat to scratch a man to death!' What others see as tragedy is for Iago an exercise in pest control. His plot, he says, is a little web in which he intends to trap a great fly – initially Cassio, ultimately Othello. This comparative zoology maddens Lear. Cradling Cordelia, he demands 'Why should a dog, a horse, a rat have life, / And thou no breath at all?' Our answer might be another question, which none of the appalled witnesses dares to ask: Why not?

For all its pitiless and sometimes unbearable honesty, Shakespearean drama does reach beyond tragedy. At the end of every performance, actors resiliently recover from death, casting doubt on its finality. Falstaff fakes his death on the battlefield in *Henry IV*, then after listening to Hal's elegy for him scrambles to his feet and drags off the corpse of Hotspur, whom he claims to have killed. In an exercise of white magic, Prospero commands graves to let forth their sleepers; Aaron's malicious exhumations in *Titus Andronicus* count as black magic. Leonato in *Much Ado About Nothing*, informed of Hero's death, regrets that he cannot tell Claudio to 'bid my daughter live', because 'That were impossible'. But Thaisa in *Pericles* is removed from her coffin 'to blow / Into life's flower again', after which she is 'buried / A second time' by being clasped in her husband's arms. In *All's Well That Ends Well* Diana riddlingly declares that 'one that's dead is quick' and immediately resolves the paradox by producing Helena, thought to be dead but actually quick with Bertram's child.

During the rural festival in *The Winter's Tale*, a discussion about crossbred flowers concludes that art can 'mend nature – change it rather' by adding to its variety. In the chapel that houses Hermione's statue, art's perfection taunts sickly, fallible nature, and dares us to believe in the better world the sculptor has designed. Paulina, guiding Leontes through the passage from life to death and back again, says 'It is required / You do awake your faith' – a command that counters Prospero's loss of faith when he ends his revels. Tormented by the unfeeling replica of his dead wife, Leontes protests that 'we are mocked with art': no image can make up for the loss of a loved one. But as he inspects the statue, he notes that 'the fixture of her eye has motion in't', which echoes the Poet's tribute to the Painter in *Timon of Athens*, and he begins to wonder if Hermione's 'sainted spirit' could 'again possess her corpse, and on this stage'. Cordelia's breath does not moisten the mirror, as Lear hopes it will; Leontes, however, cries 'O, she's warm!' when he discovers that cold stone is actually flesh.

Even so, he still assumes that this is magic, and wishes that it could be 'lawful as eating'. His startling phrase ponders a mystery: the humble, habitual physical process that sustains us is a law of life, and during religious rites it allows us to commune with the world of spirit by eating and drinking metaphorically. But is the faith that Paulina asks for no more than Coleridge's 'willing suspension of disbelief', which makes us voluntary dupes, credulous victims of art? A theatrical trick cannot close the gap between being and not being. Rather than relying on Paulina's numinous abracadabra, it might be wise to take better care of the existence that has been awarded to us. When Gloucester falls from the supposed cliff, Edgar marvels at his survival and tells him that 'Thy life's a miracle'. Comedy validates a miracle that is as lawful as breathing, and protects it from violation by tragedy's self-destructive zealots, who prefer what Hegel called 'an unhappy blessedness'.

*

The individable scene has room for the chaos of history and also for outlandish adventures in geography, with snatched views of the circumambient world. Although there is no evidence that Shakespeare travelled abroad, his characters are forever straining at the stage's limits. Claudius even comes up with an unctuous rationale for tourism when he says that he is sending Hamlet to England in the hope that 'the seas and countries different / With variable objects' will cure his malady.

The history plays ignore the unity of place by straying across the length and breadth of the kingdom. Characters elsewhere have bolder ambitions, even if they never make the excursions they have in mind. 'There's livers out of Britain,' says Imogen in *Cymbeline*, as if musing about life on other planets; Pisanio is glad she will seek refuge in an 'other place'. Restless men wander off, as Panthino notes in *The Two Gentlemen of Verona*, 'to discover islands far away'. Helena in *All's Well That Ends Well* explains her infatuation with Bertram by likening herself, 'religious in mine error', to an Indian who worships the unreciprocating sun. In *The Merry Wives of Windsor*, Falstaff imperially likens Page's wife to 'a region in Guiana, all gold and bounty', and Benedick extravagantly offers 'to go on the slightest errand now to the Antipodes', with a stop in 'the furthest inch of Asia' to fetch a souvenir toothpick. Travelling like this can be done imaginatively, with no need to go anywhere.

Rosalind tells time by measuring space, and hustles Celia by saying that 'one inch of delay more is a South-sea of discovery', as wearisome as an ocean voyage. Conversely, Antonio in *The Tempest* calculates that news of the crime he intends to commit will not travel from Naples to Tunis 'till new-born chins / Be rough and razorable'. As if elongated by perspective, like the anamorphic skull in Holbein's painting *The Ambassadors*, individual bodies stretch into a remote distance: when the smug Malvolio smiles, his face puckers into 'more lines than is in the new map with the augmentation of the Indies'. Elizabethan cartography is a challenge to Shakespeare, because those brave new worlds must surely contain novel people, like the lunar inhabitants or Martians in H. G. Wells's science fiction. Gonzalo is not surprised by Prospero's monstrously shaped accomplices, since in his youth he believed there were 'such men / Whose heads stood in their breasts'; Caliban, a taxonomic puzzle, is classified as a moon-calf, a true Shakespearean original.

The stage's overflow includes characters so vividly described that they hardly need to appear. In *The Rape of Lucrece*, the heroine studies a painting of Troy in which Achilles is represented by his spear, 'himself behind', while elsewhere

> A hand, a foot, a face, a leg, a head
> Stood for the whole to be imagined.

Without such visual clues, Romeo verbally sketches the tattered, skeletal Mantuan apothecary who has a tortoise, a stuffed alligator and 'other skins / Of ill-shaped fishes' hanging in his Dickensian shop, and Hotspur mimics a mincing, perfumed popinjay who uses snuff to block the stench of the battlefield. Also in *Henry IV*, a single line of reminiscence brings to life and then kills off poor obscure Robin Ostler, who 'never joyed since the price of oats rose; it was the death of him'. Sometimes a Homerically strenuous offstage battle is fought all over again in a speech that recounts it.

The Captain reports that Macbeth and Banquo 'bathe in reeking wounds' and 'memorize another Golgotha': war is for them a macabre, sacrilegious orgy. Posthumus reports on Cymbeline's last stand against the Roman legions, where Belarius and his two sons – the only members of a scant stage army – save the day by multiplying themselves in a flailing display of superabundant energy:

> These three,
> Three thousand confident, in act as many
> (For three performers are the file when all
> The rest do nothing).

The Gentleman who reports on the coronation in *Henry VIII* describes not a crowd but a polymorphous crush that would never fit onstage. Westminster Abbey, he says, was so tightly packed and stifling that 'a finger / Could not be wedg'd in more'. People cheer by hurling hats and cloaks into the air, 'and had their faces / Been loose, this day they had been lost'. Identities blur or are merged by his words, so men lose track of their wives because 'all were woven / So strangely in one piece', like bodies threaded together in a tapestry. Suffocation, self-dismemberment, a quest for missing persons and, as the Gentleman adds, a somewhat rank odour – all this is evidence of a jubilation that is not so much communal as cosmic: we withdraw from the personal pre-occupations of drama and look back at a world of interchangeable creatures, excitedly swarming like microbes in a drop of water.

Along with this exhilarating expansiveness, the focus of the plays can suddenly and sharply contract. Menenius in *Coriolanus* scales down the round earth when he calls his face 'the map of my microcosm', which warns the plebeians to watch for fretful wrinkles or seismic faults. No detail is too finicky to escape linguistic attention. Gower, the narrator in *Pericles*, sees Marina's 'needle wound / The cambric' as she stitches, and because the verb inflicts pain he adds that she makes the cloth 'more sound / By hurting it'. She is more tender and solicitous than Cleopatra, who fancies dangling her 'bended hook' in the river to pinion the 'slimy jaws' of fish. Shakespeare, using language to pick out minutiae that would be invisible to a theatre audience, even supplies close-ups of his characters' scalps. Antony's follicles replicate the exchange of insults between Rome and Egypt:

> My very hairs do mutiny, for the white
> Reprove the brown for rashness, and they them
> For fear and doting.

The ghost warns Hamlet that his story will cause 'each particular hair to stand on end, / Like quills upon the fretful porcupine', and Gertrude sees her son's 'bedded hair, like life in excrements, / Start up' when the spectre reappears in her private closet. Thoughts either pierce the scalp to bristle like barbs, or writhe in an imitation of vitality that is all the nastier because, in a scene that vents Hamlet's sexual disgust, the foul mess is said by Gertrude to be growing from a bed.

This miniaturizing vision pulverizes people, and reveals our world to be a loose amalgam of crumbly specks. In his anger Troilus reduces Cressida to

> The fractions of her faith, orts of her love,
> The fragments, scraps, the bits, and greasy reliques
> Of her o'er-eaten faith,

with the synonyms hammering at her almost physically until only what King John calls clods and modules remain. A senator to whom Timon of Athens owes money complains about 'his fracted dates': broken promises become fractured days, as time is chopped and sliced. The same decomposition overtakes the earth when Macbeth imagines 'nature's germens' – the seeds from which, according to Lucretius, the maternal organism grew – tumbling together in a destructive riot. Florizel in *The Winter's Tale* is equally apocalyptic: if he should ever betray Perdita, he predicts that 'the sides o' the earth' would be squeezed tight to 'mar the seeds within'. In comedy, Dumaine in *All's Well That Ends Well* wishes that Bertram could see his low company 'anatomized', which means analytically cut up, broken down into its constituents. In tragedy, Lear is more explicitly surgical. 'Let them anatomize Regan,' he says, to find if there is 'any cause in nature that makes these hard hearts'.

Anatomy, at least in its etymology, exposes atoms to scrutiny, and several characters pore over the smallest units of nature, so-called because they are indivisible. Mercutio says that Queen Mab's chariot is drawn by 'little atomi', and Phebe in *As You Like It* notices that when soft, squashy eyes are menaced by bombarding motes of dust they 'shut their coward gates on atomies'. The view from the cliff in *King Lear* is another exercise in atomizing. Crows, Edgar says, dwindle to beetles, fishermen on the beach to mice; a man gathering samphire halfway down the cliff is 'no bigger than his head'; a boat offshore is the size of its dinghy, and the actual dinghy could be a buoy.

These weirdly precise measurements are a kind of sorcery, systematically shrinking people and things, as Mercutio does in his description of Mab and her equipage. Or is life retracting, squeezing into itself for safety's sake? The Fool tells Lear to imitate the snail withdrawing into its shell, where its horns cannot be tugged or plucked by its daughters. Such images recur in the plays, always pointing with alarm to the fragility of life and the brittleness of the great globe itself. Edgar expects that Gloucester would have 'shivered like an egg' after his fall; a murderer calls Macduff's young son 'you egg' before stabbing him. More positively, Mercutio says that Romeo's head is crammed with ardour and argumentation just as 'an egg is full of meat'. But as Fortinbras marches to war over a worthless patch of ground, Hamlet wonders why men are prepared to die 'even for an eggshell'. Hamlet's own hiding place, the cerebral universe he occupies, has tougher walls, and is almost a wooden O: 'I could be bounded in a nutshell,' he tells Guildenstern, 'and count myself a king of infinite space.' At once populated and solitary, a realm and a prison, this capsule or receptacle is as flexible as the stage, which for Shakespeare was both an uproarious, conflict-ridden macrocosm and a private mental microcosm.

Carlyle regretted that Shakespeare dwindled into 'the Manager of a Playhouse, so that he could live without begging'. Romantic bardolaters wished that he had written poetic epics, verbal symphonies, or cosmic fantasias like Byron's *Manfred* or Shelley's *Prometheus Unbound* – anything but plays. He was cramped, they thought, by his chosen form: Charles Lamb argued that *King Lear* was 'impossible to be represented on a stage', because its elemental upheavals would be trivialized by the theatre's 'contemptible machinery'. Goethe went so far as to declare that Shakespeare 'never thought of the stage; it was far too narrow for his great mind; nay, the whole visible world was too narrow'.

The truth is that Shakespeare's unlimited poems swell to contain storms, crowds, clashing armies, then constrict to single out an insect or an atom, the incision made by a sewing needle or the hairs on someone's head; and the stage suits that great mind because it is where we hear and see living people use words to construct personal worlds, showing how we humanize the space in which we find ourselves and demonstrating both our need for art and its ultimate futility. 'For the law of writ and the liberty,' the Elsinore players say of themselves, 'these are the only men.' Shakespeare flouts classical laws about drama, and some of his characters deride written authority and its prescriptive texts. But for the liberty – of elastic form and tragicomically disparate content, stretched to make room for all the contradictions of our experience – he is the only man.

Words, Words, Words

Neologisms
Vocabulary as character
The working-house of thought
Vox
Ear versus eye
Shakespearean silence

In John Madden's film *Shakespeare in Love* the young dramatist is first glimpsed scrawling on scraps of paper that he crumples up and tosses away in frustration. It's a surprising sight, since Shakespeare reputedly never blotted a line, but these are not the labour pains of a play or poem: he is experimenting with ways of spelling his name. Would Shakespere, Shakespear, Shakspeare and Shackspeare smell as sweet? Being protean, he is entitled to any of those variants, all of which were current during his lifetime. Or he could make his selection from a friskier list that, thanks to Tom Stoppard's script, includes Shakesbean, Shakesbee, Shakepen and Sgagsbeard. His language is as plastic as his characters – supple, unfixed, able to be shaped and stretched.

The deletions Shakespeare makes in the film are not a symptom of writer's block. He was never stuck for words: if one did not come readily, he made another up – he invented roughly 1,700 of them. Some he must have seized on at random; others were more deliberately designed to formulate a new idea. When he altered current usage, the purpose was often to articulate the involutions of a character's thoughts and the crush of his or her feelings.

One such word is 'incarnadine', the verb Macbeth uses when he imagines staining 'the multitudinous seas' with the gore he wants to wash from his hands. It stands out because it serves such a complex purpose, relieving Macbeth but also incriminating him. It detaches him from murder by aestheticizing the evidence: elsewhere he calls Duncan's shed blood golden, and here he emphasizes its carnation shade, employing a fancy term for a pigment that interior decorators now say is rich and sumptuous, not reeking of slaughter. The aim is cathartic: purgation through poetic circumlocution – though Macbeth lets slip a blunter synonym when he imagines the incarnadined seas stained 'one red'. And despite his efforts to think pictorially or chromatically, the rawness of butchered flesh obtrudes, because the etymology of 'incarnadine' goes back to the Latin word for meat. There is also a taunting hint of Christ's incarnation, because the flesh that Macbeth has savaged ought to be a tabernacle for the spirit. The harder he tries to lave or sanitize a scene he wants to forget, the more insistently his language regurgitates these foul or doom-laden associations.

With so many conflicting impulses packed into it, 'incarnadine' is a mouthful. It does not trip lightly off the tongue, as Hamlet recommends when lecturing the players about their diction; it has to be blurted out, and a great actor will make it the physical symptom of a mental and moral state. The critic Harold Hobson remembered that Olivier uttered the phrase with a 'greasy' tone, 'slippery with an immense revulsion'. Launched into metaphorical territory by his enunciation, it conveyed the seasick nausea of his instantly awakened conscience.

Lady Macbeth has an unwieldy word of her own, which she makes up but refuses to apply to herself. Resisting any weakness that might keep her from killing, she scornfully refers to the 'compunctious visitings of nature'. The uncolloquial adjective sounds alien and obtrusive, and its consonants – before the sibilant hissing of the noun that follows – require careful negotiation when it is voiced; this ensures that she will resist the appeal of the compunction she despises. It further sabotages any appeal to compassion by flourishing a small, underhand threat that belies its professed meaning. 'Compunctious' is a weaponized word: its second syllable derives from the Latin for point or puncture, so the coinage blackly jokes that we are stabbed into feeling the moral scruples Lady Macbeth derides. 'Visitings', the noun that her adjective qualifies, further estranges her from humane nature, which is here not resident within but comes intrusively from outside, like the knocking at the castle gate after Duncan's murder. Again an entire drama contracts into a single word, and the pressure of so many compacted meanings is explosive.

overleaf
Joseph Fiennes in *Shakespeare in Love.*

No dictionary deterred Shakespeare from such inventions: he was a maker of language, not merely a user. As a lexicographer, Samuel Johnson settled on definitions that kept words in their proper places. Double meanings for Johnson amounted to misdemeanours, and his notes to the plays often castigate Shakespeare's novelties or his vulgarities. Wordplay can indeed be seditious – a verbal licence that reinforces the free-for-all of dramatic action. In *Henry VIII* the Old Lady teases Anne Boleyn with a bawdy coinage. When Anne swears that she would not want to be queen 'for all the world', the sarcastic beldame wagers that 'for little England, / You'd venture an emballing'. The spelling of that last word bothered eighteenth-century editors, some of whom preferred to read it as 'empalling', as if Anne were being ceremonially clad in the robes of state, or 'embailing', which would mean that she is being clasped by the king in an embrace that might possibly be chaste. The pun suggests all that and more, as it makes coronation and consummation (which has already occurred) overlap. The kingdom narrows to a bed, in which Anne deliciously curls up into a ball to be invested with a coarse phallic version of the sovereign's orb, one of the emblems listed in *Henry V* when the king remembers receiving 'the balm, the sceptre, and the ball' during his enthronement.

But here too, in Henry V's sober meditation on the eve of Agincourt, words misbehave. After this phrase, he tabulates the other attributes of monarchy, which include 'the sword, the mace, the crown imperial', and then acknowledges that the ritual has conferred on him a 'farcèd title'. The word that made a monarch of him is, as a French cook would say, 'farcie', artificially distended with forcemeat; the witty king here comes close to calling himself a sausage. He also implies that his rank is farcical, since the kind of buffoonery known as farce was first called that because it was seen as stuffing, having been coarsely crammed into performances of medieval liturgical plays. Shakespearean words are no respecters of etiquette, whether at court or in church.

Vocabulary is character. Othello, preparing to kill Desdemona – or, as he says with his customary high-toned flair, to put out her light – reminds himself that no 'Promethean heat' will 'relume' the spark he has extinguished. The curious verb backs up his invocation of Prometheus, who stole fire from the gods and made it his bequest to the race of men he created. Life is light, and light is warmth; Desdemona personifies this luminosity, and if the prefix 're-' sounds awkward, that is because the second chance that it might try to bring about is impossible. Ulysses in *Troilus and Cressida* strengthens his discourse on degree by claiming that, when hierarchy collapses, 'each thing meets / In mere oppugnancy'. 'Opposition' would have said the same, but less forcefully: the Latin root gives the new term a pugnacity that is stressed by stop sounds like that hard, aggressive 'g', so that the word enacts his idea.

Words like these make motives audible, and almost qualify as dramatic agents. In *Troilus and Cressida* again, after Hector refuses to continue his combat with his relative Ajax, he makes a preening boast in the third person and says that 'Not Neoptolemus so mirable / ... could promise to himself / A thought of added honour torn from Hector'. Neoptolemus – the son of Achilles, born from his liaison with the nymph Deidamia – is himself a neologism, as his name means 'new war'. But the adjective attached to him is equally remarkable: more than saying that Neoptolemus is admirable, it makes him 'mirabilis', an object of wonder, and thus indirectly serves Hector's self-mythologizing. The word might almost be a nickname, which it became when Congreve called the hero of his comedy *The Way of the World* Mirabell – a dandy who is admired by the belles of fashionable London and also by himself.

Shakespeare's characters share his verbal connoisseurship. When Polonius asks what he is reading, Hamlet replies 'Words, words, words', as if it matters only secondarily who wrote them or what they mean; he too enjoys juggling words of every kind, as when he uses 'quietus' and 'bodkin' – an elevated Latinate term for merciful death and the humdrum utensil that can bring it about – in the same sentence. 'He words me, girls', Cleopatra complains after Octavius tries to cajole her into submission. She need not fear being double-talked or shouted down: her own verbal resources extend from the sublime to the brusquely slangy. Feste in *Twelfth Night* indignantly explains that he is not employed by Olivia as a fool but as 'her corrupter of words'. He sees this as an honourable profession, and any writer who uses language for connotation rather than meagre denotation might agree. Words are only too happy to be led astray, and have little sense of obligation to the objects they label. As Feste explains, they 'are very rascals since bonds disgraced them': he means that our spoken word should be our bond, and scorns the reliance on written contracts. Preferring lively speech to the dead letters of a text, Shakespeare unbound words and rejoiced in their rascality.

*

The 'omnipresent creativeness' of Shakespeare, which Coleridge likened to that of 'the Spinozistic deity', bursts forth in the rampant vigour of his language. The analogy with the teeming abundance that Spinoza found in nature is not misplaced. In the Bible, God is the Word; chaos acquires form when the creator speaks. Shakespeare's characters take over from there. The lungs of these people inflate the globe and speed it on its rounds with what Hamlet calls the 'windy suspiration' of their breathing. They ensure that the world exists by describing it, and keep it in existence by unstoppably talking. Speech counts as a vital sign, evidence of spirit: as Gertrude says to Hamlet, 'words [are] made of breath, / And breath of life'.

The fecundity of Shakespeare's language even quickens descriptions of death and disaster. In *The Comedy of Errors*, Egeon says that the wrecked ship on which he lost his wife and sons was 'sinking-ripe': its mishap becomes a kind of fulfilment, and in the fullness of time, on this very day, those he thought dead will indeed be restored to him alive. When Salarino jokes about the capsizing of Antonio's ship in *The Merchant of Venice* he imagines the mast turning upside down 'to kiss her burial'. In a calmer nautical context, metaphor becomes a fertilizing agent. In *A Midsummer Night's Dream*, Titania remembers that she and her votaress would stand on the beach and laugh as they watched the sails of trading vessels 'conceive / And grow big-bellied in the wanton wind'. The image voices a repressed sadness: her companion later died in childbirth. No harm comes to the 'great-bellied women' squashed into the over-crowded Abbey in *Henry VIII*, who use their swollen stomachs 'like rams / In the old time of war' – rotund battering rams that peaceably part the throng.

Shakespearean language adds value to whatever it denominates. Valentine in *Two Gentlemen of Verona* jokes that the only treasure of the down-at-heel Thurio is his 'exchequer of words'; expending his own linguistic wealth on Silvia, Valentine feels

> as rich in having such a jewel
> As twenty seas, if all their sand were pearl,
> The water nectar and the rocks pure gold.

Love is judged by the spendthrift verbal superfluity it provokes. At their first meeting, Romeo recites a prepared compliment, to which Juliet responds with a quatrain of her own. They continue with exactly matched antiphonal lines that add up into a sonnet, after which they 'kiss by th' book'. Hate or contempt are equally eloquent. Enobarbus reels off a succession of synonyms to describe the sycophancy of Lepidus, interjecting snorts that are more expressive or expletive than his words:

> Hoo! Hearts, tongues, figures, scribes, bards, poets cannot
> Think, speak, cast, write, sing, number – hoo! –
> His love to Antony.

The poet William Carlos Williams found in Shakespeare's language 'a namelessness of unprecedented freedom'. Namelessness perhaps refers to his nominalism – the separability of words from things, which is responsible for the unfurling menu of signatures in *Shakespeare in Love*. Confusion dogs Rosencrantz and Guildenstern, a like-minded pair of time-servers who are differentiated only by their names. Claudius and Gertrude seem unsure about which of them is which, and diplomatically apply a genteel adjective first to one and then to the other so that neither will feel slighted. He says 'Thanks, Rosencrantz and gentle Guildenstern'; she chimes in with 'Thanks, Guildenstern and gentle Rosencrantz.' 'O Romeo, Romeo, wherefore art thou Romeo?' asks Juliet, who wishes he could 'refuse thy name', the badge of his enmity to her clan; he asks Friar Laurence 'In what vile part of this anatomy / Doth my name lodge?', denying that it organically belongs to him. The soothsayer in *Cymbeline* is less of an essentialist. Instructed to interpret the oracle's prediction that 'a lion's whelp shall… be embraced by a piece of tender air', he does so by exercising a slick etymological sleight of hand. He first identifies Posthumus Leonatus as the lion's whelp, 'being *leonatus*', which is self-evident. He then takes a giddier hermeneutic risk. Imogen, he declares, is the 'piece of tender air'

> Which we call *mollis aer*; and *mollis aer*
> We term it *mulier*, which *mulier* I divine
> Is this most constant wife.

Cymbeline's guarded response is 'This hath some seeming': the tone of his voice and the expression on his face are left up to the actor.

A coinage – in itself a beautifully poetic metaphor, tallying words as tokens of value – can be plucked from nowhere, as when Enobarbus invites the damp night to 'disponge' on him. Because the language had not yet been codified, Shakespeare could re-assign words to new categories. A noun becomes an adjective, an adjective a verb: Achilles is 'kingdom'd', Cressida says that her grief 'violenteth'. Sometimes an adjective swallows its accompanying noun, as when Menenius asks the citizens for 'a small – of what you have little', meaning patience. Diminutives are a form of condescension or patronage: further belittling what is already small, the patrician here whittles down the self-esteem of the plebeians. Cleopatra deploys a noun as a participle when she swears that Octavius never 'shall / Be brooched with me', which announces her refusal to be taken to Rome as his ornament or captive trophy. Re-enlivening a dead metaphor, her word has a barb in it. 'Brooch' derives from a medieval variant of 'broach', referring to a skewer or even to Hamlet's bodkin; because it is secured by a pin, it serves in French as the name of a spit, called a brochette. Anglicized, it has a similarly pointed function: to broach a difficult subject is to prod the conversation in a different direction. Cleopatra is using it figuratively, to stab or prick her conqueror. Johnson aptly called the quibble Shakespeare's 'fatal Cleopatra for which he lost the world'; she is herself a practised quibbler.

Words seem to germinate, as Hamlet says the sun breeds maggots in a dead dog. There is a punning frisson when Claudius tells Laertes about the French cavalier Lamond, who was almost 'incorpsed and demi-natured' with his horse. The idea is that they were incorporated in each other, but because Claudius is plotting Hamlet's death his coinage unmasks him by producing a corpse. Reports of Laertes' prowess at fencing, he goes on, 'did Hamlet so envenom with his envy'. Here the metaphor could be subliminally prompting Laertes to suggest that the foil should be dipped in poison – or has Shakespeare, his mind racing, got ahead of his characters? Cheating appearances are maintained: on the surface, all Claudius means is that is Hamlet is self-poisoned by jealousy.

When Timon, grubbing in the earth, speaks of its 'conceptious womb', he might be describing Shakespeare's brain and its teeming brood of verbal conceits and intellectual concepts. Characters verbalize thought extemporally, as Shakespeare probably did when writing. Othello, having told the senators about 'hills whose heads touch heaven', inverts the metaphor and fictitiously peoples the landscape with monsters by claiming that he also encountered 'men whose heads / Do grow beneath their shoulders'. Reading or listening, we can sense one word or image giving birth to another. Troilus, needing a new term for an embrace that is desperately tight, speaks of his 'embrasures' with Cressida, which sounds almost architectural; a little later, Hector and Ajax solemnize a more political 'embracement'. Pirates in *Antony and Cleopatra* 'ear and wound' the sea with their ships – an incongruous agricultural image, which visualizes the keel as a ploughshare and assumes that waves can feel pain. Not long after this, Agrippa applies the metaphor to Caesar, Cleopatra and their child Cesarion, healing the rift when he says 'He ploughed her, and she cropped'.

Although they seem to start into life spontaneously, inventions like these are psychological giveaways, because they show how characters modify or modulate the facts to suit themselves. Lady Macbeth speaks of sharpening her 'keen knife' for a prospective murder, but more squeamishly asks that it 'see not the wound it makes'. Personifying the weapon, she turns it into a witness, as if it were committing the crime of its own volition but – in a transposition of her own mixed motives – with averted eyes. She also flinches when she forbids heaven to 'peep through the blanket of the dark' to restrain her: blankets are comforting, and they soften the violence she thinks she is capable of committing. Imogen envies the 'senseless linen' of the handkerchief that Posthumus waves as he sails away, and Pisanio reports that his glove and hat also signalled, expressing 'the fits and stirs of 's mind'. Those items of clothing are extensions of the body: how else can we communicate when we are too far away to speak? Such images are specimens of what John Ruskin called the 'pathetic fallacy', a view of the external world distorted by our feelings – but in Shakespeare they impart emotional truth, not sentimental falsehood. Gertrude says that Ophelia drowned because an 'envious sliver' of the branch that supported her broke, after which her thirsty garments, 'heavy with their drink', dragged her down. Transferring blame to the tree and then to Ophelia's dress, she pacifies Laertes by portraying his sister's suicide as an accident; perhaps – given the literary veneer applied to her narrative – she is also preparing an evasive public statement. The little fallacies tell us more about her sense of complicity than neutral facts ever could.

*

Don Armado, the combustible Spaniard in *Love's Labour's Lost*, prides himself on using 'fire-new words', which he might have freshly plucked from what the Chorus in *Henry V* calls 'the quick forge and working-house of thought'. As this industrial image suggests, language in Shakespeare is almost eruptive, and it can scorch or sear. The breath of the fulminating heroine in *The Rape of Lucrece* is like smoke from Etna or fumes discharged by a cannon. Benedick is glad that Beatrice's breath is not as terrible as the sarcastic words it forms, or else 'she would infect to the north star'. Hotspur laughs at the physiology of utterance when he likens the huffing and puffing of Glendower to the way 'our grandam earth' belches to relieve 'the imprisoning of unruly wind / Within her womb'.

More formally, Shakespeare's plays put words through their paces, often almost militarizing them. The senators in *Timon of Athens*, craving noisy pomp, think of language strutting on parade; they tell Timon that his words will 'become your lips as they pass through them', doing him honour, and they wait for his pronouncements to 'enter in our ears like great triumphers / In their applauding gates'. He resists, because false words are 'a cantherizing to the root o' th' tongue' – burning and drying it up. Taciturn Cordelia, challenged to compete with the protestations of filial love made by her sisters, suppresses the flow and stops the automated march. Verbiage for her is vomit, which is why she 'cannot heave my heart / Into my mouth'.

Into the mouth and out through the lips – this, for Shakespeare, is almost a rite of passage, activating words dramatically. 'You must allow *vox*,' says Feste, who insists on performing Malvolio's aggrieved letter rather than tamely reading it out. Gloucester in *Henry VI* keeps a written record of a treacherous bishop's crimes, but is ready 'verbatim to rehearse the method of my pen'. Told of the king's displeasure, Wolsey in *Henry VIII* demands document-ation, because 'Words cannot carry / Authority so weighty'. His request is a symptom of weakness: in Shakespeare's plays, voiced words are always worth more than the paper they are written on. Henry V resonantly declares that we survive in history only if our successors 'with full mouth / Speak freely of our acts'. Otherwise, as he puts it in an image that equates silence with mutilation or emasculation, 'our grave, / Like Turkish mute, shall have a tongueless mouth'. For a veteran of Agincourt, Henry predicts, the names of his commanders and comrades will be 'familiar in his mouth as household words'. Then, switching to prosaic banter when he woos the French princess, he scoffs at 'fellows of infinite tongue' who know how to rhyme, and says that 'a speaker is but a prater' – a moment of mock-modesty that resembles Othello's disclaimer when he tells the senators 'Rude am I in my speech'.

Wrenchingly, Lear's elegy for Cordelia praises her voice, 'ever soft, / Gentle and low', and now stilled. Coriolanus addresses his mousy wife as 'my gracious silence'; her talking is done for her by Volumnia, who promises that when Rome burns 'I'll speak a little'. Emilia in *Othello* is ordered by Iago to 'Speak within door', but she finds a voice as we watch and listen. At last, perhaps emboldened by what Desdemona calls 'my free speech', she resolves to 'speak as liberal as the north', associating her breath with a chilly, boisterous gale, and she dominates the play's conclusion when she rails at Othello and exposes Iago. Stabbed for her pains, she repeats a snatch of Desdemona's ballad and then, having finally made herself heard, decides to end in speech not song: 'I speak true. So, speaking as I think, alas, I die.'

Power is vocal. Jack Cade, who leads a populist revolt in *Henry VI*, persecutes literacy. He condemns a clerk as a traitor because he can write his name, reviles grammarians who 'talk of a noun and a verb and other such abominable words as no Christian ear can endure to hear', damns lawyers for slaughtering lambs to make parchment, and berates Lord Saye, who 'caused printing to be used and… built a paper-mill'. Once all archives and legal records are burned, Cade declares 'My mouth shall be the Parliament of England.' He has the etymology on his side: a parliament is a place for parleying, a talking shop. To become a consul, Coriolanus needs not votes but 'voices' – the acclaim of the plebeians – and he enlists the tribunes because they are officially 'tongues o' th' common mouth'. When their cheerleading fails, he leans harder on the metaphor and makes it dental: our faces have a built-in weapon, made for gnashing and gnawing. 'You being their mouths, why rule you not their teeth?' he snaps.

On his return from battle, Coriolanus needs no prompters, and the tribune Brutus reports that 'All tongues speak of him, and the blearèd sights / Are spectacled to see him'. Anecdotes about the mob's agitation keep to that re-ordering of the senses. Rumoured acclaim takes precedence, while vision, which now needs prosthetic help, follows in second place. Brutus notes that a nurse 'chats him', or prattles about him; only then does he add that a kitchen wench clambers the walls 'to eye him'. Volumnia, advising Coriolanus how to present himself to the citizens in the marketplace, adheres to the same order of priority for her own disdainful reasons: 'Action is eloquence, and the eyes of th' ignorant / More learned than the ears.' She tells him to cultivate what a politician today would call his 'image' by abasing himself like a mulberry tree loaded with fruit; sound bites should not be wasted on the mob.

Other characters, dealing with auditors who are less oafish, can rely on words alone. Boult in *Pericles* does not exhibit the new woman he has recruited for his brothel. Instead he says 'I have drawn her picture with my voice', perhaps because adjectives are a part of speech that specializes in titillation. Othello remembers that, during his early visits to her father's house, Desdemona's 'greedy ear' would 'devour up' his traveller's tales. Endowed with an appetite, the organ is not a passive receptor; like a displaced mouth, it hungrily forages for words to ingest.

Leonardo da Vinci, as a visual artist, argued that 'hearing is less noble than sight': the ear cannot retain sounds, whereas objects studied by the eye can acquire permanence as graphic images. Shakespeare saw – or rather heard – the world differently. Lear commands Gloucester to read a letter and 'mark but the penning'. Gloucester says he cannot since his eye sockets are empty, but for Lear that is no disqualification: 'Look with thine ears', he says. We do exactly that when, on level, empty boards far from the sea, Edgar terrifies us with his vertiginous account of the cliff at Dover. Even in his narrative poems, Shakespeare emphasizes the oral and auditory rather than the textual. 'What! canst thou talk? Hast thou a tongue?' marvels Venus, who has previously mocked the bashful, tight-lipped Adonis as 'Thing like a man'. He vows not to succumb, even if the goddess entreats him with 'twenty thousand tongues'; her only solace is the 'verbal repetition' of the echoes that multiply her twenty laments twenty times over. After being ravished by Tarquin, Lucrece calls for paper, ink and pen, intending to send her husband an appeal for help. She then decides not to write to him after all, because she might be maligned by gossip. Writing is a kind of defilement, and

> To shun this blot, she would not blot the letter
> With words, till action might become them better.

Spoken words disappear harmlessly into air; marked or scratched on a page they become injurious. When Hamlet writes, it is to compose a literal death sentence for Rosencrantz and Guildenstern. His penmanship, he says, used to have a fashionably slovenly negligence. Now he takes pains to write clearly, and he is punctilious about punctuation, arguing that the execution of his former friends will 'stand a comma' to fill in any diplomatic gap between England and Denmark.

For such characters, the paraphernalia of writing are at best unnatural, at worst deathly. 'I loved my books,' says Prospero, a little regretfully: his preoccupation with them made possible the plot against his dukedom. The moribund King John calls himself 'a scribbled form, drawn with a pen / Upon a parchment'. The pen's incisions are useless surgery; his skin has been parched by the heat of the poison that makes his bowels, as he complains, crumble to dust. 'Their cheeks are paper,' says Henry V of the blanched traitors he ensnares. Othello sees Desdemona's skin as 'this fair paper, this most goodly book', then charges that it was 'made to write "whore" upon'. Leonato in *Much Ado About Nothing*, convinced of his daughter's impurity, says she has 'fall'n / Into a pit of ink'. Olivia rejects the lovelorn appeal that Viola delivers from Orsino by referring to it as 'your text' and claiming to have already read it. Benedick grumbles that Claudio, who 'was wont to speak plain', has 'turned orthography' after falling in love. Indifference to standardized spelling – apparently shared by Shakespeare – hints at the affinity between Benedick and Beatrice: according to Hero, she ignores a suitor's obvious merits and prefers to jumble up his features and 'spell him backward'. Nathaniel in *Love's Labour's Lost* regrets that Dull the constable 'hath not eat paper' or 'drunk ink'; he is lucky to be illiterate if he escapes such a diet. On his deathbed, Falstaff's nose is 'sharp as a pen'. That counts as a terminal symptom, though he remains voluble, and Mistress Quickly reports that he 'babbled of green fields'.

Yet Shakespeare's language cannot deny its empathy to the missives people exchange. 'Leave, gentle wax,' says Edgar in *King Lear* as he surreptitiously opens a letter addressed to his brother. Aware that he is doing something unmannerly, he makes amends by apologizing to the seal that was once soft and molten, and the phrase turns a functional act into a small glimpse of his character. Albany is cooler and sharper-eyed when he hands to Goneril another letter whose contents incriminate her. 'No tearing, lady', he warns.

Whether exercised in tragic tirades or comic slanging matches, the tongue is a Shakespearean character's most precious implement. To Benedick, Beatrice is 'my Lady Tongue'. Confronted by Yorick's remains, Hamlet does not immediately notice the holes where the eyes once were or the hollow cranium: his first comment is 'That skull had a tongue in it and could sing once.' Ajax threatens to slice off the tongue of the slanderous Thersites, who replies, unintimidated, 'I shall speak as much as thou afterwards.' Kate warns Petruchio that the wasp's sting is in its tongue, though his task in taming her is to 'charm her chattering'. Don Pedro says that the forthright Benedick has 'a heart sound as a bell, and his tongue is the clapper'. Falstaff rearranges his anatomy, claiming to 'have a whole school of tongues in this belly of mine'. He knows that the tongue is an organ of taste as well as speech, and says that sherry, having invigorated the brain, is 'delivered o'er to the voice, the tongue, which is the birth', after which it is translated into 'excellent wit'. Rosaline in *Love's Labour's Lost* finds Berowne to be lingually appealing, attractive because of the way he talks. His 'fair tongue', she says, is 'conceit's expositor'.

That compliment is gloomily echoed in *Titus Andronicus* when Lavinia's rapists cut out her tongue to prevent her from identifying them. Marcus likens her tongue to a bird in the 'pretty hollow cage' of her mouth, and calls it the 'delightful engine of her thoughts, / That blabbed them with such pleasing eloquence'. Blabbing, like Falstaff's babbling of green fields, is a touching reminiscence of baby talk. Lavinia learns to write as a second-best and, guided by Marcus, uses a staff held in her mouth – a wooden tongue – to scratch the names of her attackers in the dirt. Titus has already undertaken to 'wrest an alphabet' from her body language, interpreting her moans, winks and nods.

For him the phonemes remain silent, whereas the lyrically besotted characters in *Romeo and Juliet* vocalize their way through the alphabet. Romeo derives an aria in verse from the letter O, which is the sound of a sigh and the sign for the nothingness from which he believes that love, hate, laughter and art all emerge:

> O brawling love, O loving hate,
> O anything of nothing first create!
> O heavy lightness, serious vanity,
> Misshapen chaos of well-seeming forms!

In a corresponding performance, Juliet trebles the letter I. She uses it to indicate herself but has it cancel her out if the Nurse, spelling it differently, gives her news she dreads:

> Hath Romeo slain himself? Say thou but 'Ay',
> And that bare vowel 'I' shall poison more

Than the death-darting eye of cockatrice.
I am not I if there be such an 'Ay'
Or those eyes shut that makes thee answer 'Ay'.

The Nurse plays a game of her own with a consonant. She points out that 'rosemary and Romeo begin both with a letter' and adds that R is 'the dog's name'. Ben Jonson, in his *English Grammar*, called R 'the dog's letter' because it 'hirreth in the sound' – a throaty growling that issues a warning without words; the Nurse snarls under her breath in response to Romeo's teasing. As with canine language, throat-clearing and heavy breathing in humans also warn of unnamed infractions. Leontes in *The Winter's Tale* says that, although Hermione 'deserves high speech', she is tainted by wordless innuendos, 'the shrug, the "hum" or "ha", these petty brands / That calumny doth use'.

Words so palatable almost count as a source of nutrition, as 'hot in the mouth' as ginger, for which Sir Toby in *Twelfth Night* has a taste. Even music, made of non-alimentary air, is described as food for lovers by Orsino and again by Cleopatra. When Benedick admits he loves Beatrice, she asks 'Will you not eat your word?' For once, this is no cliché: he refuses, regardless of what sauce seasons the phrase. In *Love's Labour's Lost* a boy marvels at the polylingual pedantry of Nathaniel and Holofernes, who 'have been at a great feast of languages'. The banquet can be disgusting, indigestible. Timon says that 'man with liquorish draughts / And morsels unctuous, greases his pure mind', and at the start of the play, the falsely modest Poet calls his verse 'a gum which oozes / From whence 'tis nourish'd', a slimy secretion like the 'glib and oily art' Goneril and Regan employ to flatter Lear.

For some characters, poetry could be defined as language overcooked, a dessert not a meal. A servant in *Troilus and Cressida* winces at a 'stewed phrase' uttered by Pandarus; Achilles in the same play 'bastes his arrogance with his own seam', bathing in lard. Coriolanus, more abstemious, refuses to hear himself 'dieted / In praises sauc'd with lies'. Antony sees his fall from grace in gustatory terms. He first likens his followers to grovelling spaniels, then adds that they 'discandy, melt their sweets / On blossoming Caesar'. Their compliments are drivel, a glutinous saliva, but he too undergoes dissolution. 'Discandy' contains an echo of descant: as when Richard III says he intends to 'descant on mine own deformity', it sings a counterpoint to what Antony is saying and reasserts his appetite for life's sweetness and its springtime beauty, even as he prepares to leave it.

The relish is not confined to garish terms like 'exsufflicate', the adjective Othello uses to describe the blown-up, groundless suggestion of Desdemona's infidelity when Iago first presents it to him. Once her reasoned arguments fail, Lady Anne in *Richard III* can only spit in the face of her insidious wooer, and many of Shakespeare's colloquialisms are aimed in the same way, like liquid darts. Nestor in *Troilus and Cressida* rejoices to see Hector's sword mowing down 'the strawy Greeks'. The French nobles in *Henry V* call damp Albion 'slobb'ry' and joke that its eroded outline on the map is 'nook-shotten', shot full of holes. The Duke tells Othello that he must 'slubber' or besmirch his celebrity by travelling to Cyprus to fight the Turks; equally uncourtly, Desdemona suggests to Emilia that political worries have 'puddled' her husband's brain. Iago, extorting treasures to be given supposedly to Desdemona, has 'bobbed' Roderigo, who realizes that he has been 'fopped', taken for a fool. Words like these set off small detonations, releasing a burst of energy that diminishes or destroys the people they target. As Caliban says, the benefit of having learned Prospero's language is that he knows how to curse.

Although the biblical Logos is abstract, unvoiced, human language can tire and falter, which threatens the entire Shakespearean creation that it sustains. Timon's steward Flavius blames him for ruining his estate by airily disbursing goods whenever he opens his mouth. Omit a consonant, and everything implodes into nothing:

> O my good sir, the world is but a word.
> Were it all yours to give it in a breath,
> How quickly were it gone!

When Macbeth imagines his future, with life as a prison term and time itself as a punishment, he measures duration in verbal particles that no longer add up into articulate units and are as meaninglessly repetitive as the ticking of a clock. Those vacuous tomorrows will continue, he says, 'to the last syllable of recorded time', not its last second. The end of the world is the end of words.

*

The verbal or vocal bounty dispensed by Shakespeare exceeds that of Orpheus, whose music, according to the song performed for Queen Katherine in *Henry VIII*, unfroze mountain peaks and made trees genuflect. In the Orphic myth, inanimate nature remained silent, but Shakespeare transplants tongues into objects that are obdurately dumb.

Hamlet imagines the ghost 'preaching to stones', and believes that his pallid glare could 'make them capable' – of what, he doesn't say. Macbeth asks the earth not to hear his steps as he guiltily treads on it, for fear that 'thy very stones prate of my whereabout', which has an extra force because prating is blabber, gossip, a colloquial denunciation that might come from underfoot. Later, nightmarishly outdoing Orpheus, Macbeth claims that 'stones have been known to move and trees to speak' to identify malefactors. Antony wishes there were 'a tongue in every wound of Caesar', and a metonymy at the start of *Macbeth* brings that about: as the bloody Captain faints, he says 'My gashes cry for help'. More than a rhetorical trick, this shows the Captain to be a staunch professional, whose gashes utter a plea that he will not make on his own behalf. Scarus in *Antony and Cleopatra* treats his lesions as letters, with his skin as tough parchment, and he reads them as insignia rather than letting them cry out. 'I had a wound here that was like a T,' he shrugs, 'But now 'tis made an H.' In response to a girl's blushes, John Donne suggested that her 'blood / Spoke in her cheeks' so that 'one might almost say, her body thought'. Shakespeare, less hesitant, makes speech travel to the bodily extremity furthest from the mouth. Ulysses says of Cressida 'There's language in her eye, her cheek, her lip', which all advertise availability. He then adds 'Nay, her foot speaks'.

Isabella, outwitted by Angelo in *Measure for Measure* as they bargain about Claudio's life, pleads that 'I have no tongue but one'. Kent is wilier, and in *King Lear* he disguises himself by borrowing 'other accents... / That can my speech diffuse'. The banished Valentine in *Two Gentlemen of Verona* is equally adaptable, and when the outlaws ask him 'Have you the tongues?' he pertly replies 'My youthful travel therein made me happy'. They find him useful because he is 'a linguist'. Bolingbroke in *Richard II* is mournfully monoglot, and complains that exile in France will mean estrangement from 'my native English', a kind of 'speechless death'. His son Hal is more versatile: Warwick in *Henry IV* argues that the prince keeps company with Falstaff and his scurrilous gang to study them 'like a strange tongue... to gain the language', and if he is to acquire the common touch he will need to learn 'the most immodest word'.

Complementing his tragical-comical-historical-pastoral conflation of genres, Shakespeare's language is a Babel of overlapping idioms and idiolects. Rumour, personified in the second part of *Henry IV*, wears a costume painted with multiple tongues, and Coriolanus when he scorns the electoral rights of the rabble wishes he could 'pluck out / The multitudinous tongue'.

Ben Jonson disliked the mock-medieval archaisms in *The Faerie Queene* and said that Spenser 'writ no language'; Shakespeare might have boasted that he wrote all languages, or that he made them up rather than bothering to learn them. The soldiers who trap Parolles in *All's Well That Ends Well* do so by using a Jabberwockian lingo that they invent for the occasion. 'Oscorbidulchos volivorco', says one of them. 'Boblibindo chicurmurco', says another. As with patter in an Italian comic opera, enjoyment does not require understanding.

When the choral figure of Gower in *Pericles* apologizes for making everyone in the play's eastern Mediterranean diaspora speak English, he winks at a restrictive convention that Shakespeare on occasion ignores. The princess in *Henry V* chatters and giggles in French during an English lesson that concentrates on naming the parts of the body. She warps vowels and sibilates consonants: 'neck' comes out as 'nick', 'nails' are 'mailès', 'chin' turns into 'sin'. Aghast at the gruff foreign noise, or perhaps a little aroused by her own cheeky errors, she decides – agreeing with Feste – that the words sound 'corruptible, gros, et impudique'. The Host in *The Merry Wives of Windsor* parses a title to which Falstaff has no right, regaling him and adding the Latin, Teutonic and Egyptian synonyms for his unearned status. 'Thou'rt an emperor', he says, 'Caesar, kaiser, and pheezer', turning vizier into a non-verbal snort. Later Evans the parson delivers a lecture on Latin grammar with a thick Welsh accent; Mistress Quickly adds to the confusion when she decides that 'nouns' must mean 'wounds', and announces that 'hog' – Evans's mispronounced version of the pronoun 'hoc' – refers to bacon.

Quickly's malapropisms have an inspired poetic oddity, equalled only by the word-mangling of the sodden midwife Mrs Gamp in Dickens's *Martin Chuzzlewit*. She chides Falstaff for provoking Mistress Ford into 'such a canaries', meaning quandary: canary – the name of a dance and of a yellowish wine – wishes on

Alice a reeling, drunken derangement. In *Henry IV* she tells Falstaff that he and his bawd Doll Tearsheet are 'as rheumatic as two dry toasts'. She should have said 'choleric', but has mixed up the theory of the temperamental humours. Choler is hot and dry, like toast, whereas rheum is cold and wet; rheumatism, however, suits the two ageing reprobates, and the comparison with unbuttered toast evokes the abrasion of brittle bones. Enraged, Quickly brings a legal 'exion' against Falstaff: should we think of Ixion in the Greek myth, who was expelled from Olympus for lecherously desiring the wife of Zeus and punished by being pinioned on a fiery wheel? She also denounces him as 'an infinitive thing upon my score'. Though the sum he owes her may be infinite, her adjective does more than present him with a bill. She pays tribute to Falstaff's infinitude, or to his unfailing supply of excuses and verbal evasions, and also makes a fortuitously apt point about grammar. Not yet a verb, an infinitive exists in a state of inactive poise, awaiting an action that may or may not follow: 'To be, or not to be' is the best example. Falstaff resembles an infinitive because he is inert, as massively lethargic as Hamlet is tremulously indecisive. 'Thing' – applied to Falstaff as it is to Coriolanus or Caliban or Antony's crocodile – has its own suggestiveness: creatures so congenially or malevolently monstrous belong to no class or category and are one of a kind, inimitable and incorrigible, uniquely Shakespearean.

Characters often react with amazement to events they witness, pushing language to its limits and beyond. Edgar attributes Gloucester's survival 'to the clearest gods, who make them honours / Of men's impossibilities', and when his domineering mother kneels before him Coriolanus imagines pebbles fired at the stars and rooted trees hurled at the sun, 'Murd'ring impossibility to make / What cannot be slight work'. Timon calls gold a 'visible god', admires its capacity to speak in all tongues, and says that it 'solder'st close impossibilities, / And mak'st them kiss!' Achieving the impossible is for Shakespeare the effortless task of metaphors not money, as figures of speech enable people to transcend themselves. 'I am the sea' says Titus, whose grief after the attack on Lavinia is oceanic. 'I the earth' he adds, closing the equation by omitting the verb: he is the battered ground that must absorb a downpour from 'the weeping welkin', since Lavinia is now equated with the torn, tearful sky. Imogen reaches up towards an impossibility when she receives a letter Posthumus has sent from Milford Haven. 'O for a horse with wings!' she says, and her wish – funny, touching and gloriously poetic – explains why we devised a myth in which such a creature, the aerodynamic stallion Pegasus, actually exists.

Hamlet, railing at Laertes during Ophelia's funeral, makes impossibilities the measure of a bravado that is entirely linguistic. 'Woot drink up eisel, eat a crocodile?' he rants, bragging 'I'll do't.' Eisel is vinegar, so Hamlet vaults instantly from a distasteful drinking contest to a more recondite challenge, then ends with a boast that, despite its puerility, demonstrates the far-flung reach of his thinking and the tireless derring-do of his play-acting. After this last bout of vaunting, the ever-talkative Hamlet ends in silence – at least he does so in the 1603 Quarto, although the Folio adds a phonetic cadenza in which he repeatedly enunciates a vowel that, depending on the actor's choice, can be a death rattle, a groan, or a sweet prince's melodious departing sigh: 'O, O, O, O'. Timon pronounces a more muted epitaph for himself when he says 'Lips, let four words go by, and language end.'

All the same, logocide would not entirely shut down Shakespeare's theatre. Bassanio receives 'speechless messages' from Portia's eyes, and knows how to interpret her encouraging semaphore; Troilus warns Cressida that the Greeks have 'dumb-discoursive' airs and graces. When Virginia Woolf saw *Twelfth Night* at the Old Vic in 1933, she warmed to its yearning poetry and witty prose, even though she believed that Shakespeare wrote 'too quick for the human tongue' and should be read, not listened to. Yet what moved her most was a protracted moment that does not exist on the page: the pause when the reunited twins 'stand looking at each other in a silent ecstasy'. The greatest of writers, who lavished his loquacity on all his characters, knew when words were redundant.

This Is the Forest of Arden

From crow to swan
Shakespeare reformed
Shakespeare the novelist
Concerts of one

The first reference to Shakespeare in print was an insult. In 1592 Robert Greene called him a 'Johannes factotum' – a jack of all trades, surely no bad thing in a theatre company – and an 'upstart crow', a bumptious provincial who borrowed the plumage of 'rare wits' like Greene and his university-educated cronies. After Shakespeare's death, Ben Jonson likened him to a bird of another kind, a 'sweet swan of Avon'. The raucous caricature may be nearer the mark than the euphonious compliment: Greene's reference to young 'Shake-scene' catches the disturbance caused by the writer Jonson fulsomely called 'my gentle Shakespeare'. The swan in Jonson's poetic obituary is already silent, having soared aloft to join Apollo, who installed Cygnus in the heavens. It was easy to commend a competitor when he was no longer a threat.

'Well, this is the forest of Arden', says Rosalind in *As You Like It*, clearly wishing that she were somewhere less bucolic. Shakespeare left Stratford to make his name and fortune in an art that was innately urban, connected to the court but domiciled in the unrespectable streets where theatres abutted on bawdy houses and bear pits. His elegists, however, treated him as a pastoral poet not a dramatist, and were homesick for the Midlands on his behalf. Milton acknowledged that 'sweetest Shakespeare' worked in 'tower'd cities' among 'the busy hum of men'; all the same, he called Shakespeare 'Fancy's child' and used a version of Jonson's ornithological analogy to suggest that he twittered pleasingly, 'warbling his native woodnotes wild', without perhaps having much to say. Shaw opportunistically seized on the phrase about the woodnotes, and had Professor Higgins in *Pygmalion* apply it to the alliterative blather of the dustman Doolittle, who is at least an urban rogue, not a blithe, childlike yokel. Higgins is proud of his own 'Miltonic mind': the contrast between Shakespeare and Milton sets pleasure against virtue, the human comedy against paradise regained.

In 1637 William Davenant imagined the Avon weeping for its

George Romney's *Infant Shakespeare Attended by Nature and the Passions*, engraved by John Boydell in 1797.

native son, with flowers on its banks mournfully drooping. The *Ode* recited by Garrick at the Jubilee described the muses dancing around Shakespeare on 'the green velvet' beside 'fairy-haunted Avon', and concluded by pleading that the meadows along the river should remain common land, 'unconfin'd, / As broad and general as thy boundless mind' – an ironic wish, given that Shakespeare was part owner of some fields near the town that in 1614 were lucratively enclosed for grazing sheep. Thomas Linley's *Lyric Ode on the Fairies, Aerial Beings and Witches of Shakespeare* was set to a text by French Lawrence in which Fancy, once more young Shakespeare's guardian, is commanded by Jove to protect the stripling from the 'sordid wishes of the grov'ling crowd'. That means keeping him in Stratford, where in 'Arden's inmost shade' he consorts with the 'sportive train' of phantoms that are the subjects of Linley's composition. Garrick referred to Shakespeare with matey colloquialism as 'Warwickshire Will'; in 1841 Carlyle called him 'the Warwickshire Peasant' – a yeoman, closer to the soil than Milton's sylvan naïf.

The most sacred relic of the Shakespeare cult was a tree,

SHAKESPEARE

allegedly planted by him in the garden of his house in Stratford. Garrick called it the 'Blest Mulberry', and said that it shared Shakespeare's immortality. In fact the owner of the property, annoyed by gawking tourists, chopped the mulberry down in the 1750s and sold the wood to an entrepreneur who had it carved into souvenirs, among them a series of goblets that were treasured as literary Grails. Pseudo-rural homages to Shakespeare have proliferated elsewhere. Central Park in New York has a garden planted with the flowers and herbs mentioned in the plays, including Desdemona's lachrymose willow and a white mulberry that was grafted, according to legend, from the so-called 'Parent Tree' in Stratford.

This emphasis on Shakespeare's rustic origins may explain why, when the theatres reopened in 1660 after almost two decades of puritan censorship, his work displeased fashionable London. The comedies were considered coarse, the tragedies brutish. The diarist Samuel Pepys dismissed *A Midsummer Night's Dream* as insipid, and called *Romeo and Juliet* the worst play he had ever seen. Drastic revision was needed to sophisticate Shakespeare and make him presentable again.

Davenant adapted *Macbeth* in 1663–4, writing extra songs for the witches and hoisting them aloft on flying machines, which turned the play's exploration of crime and its self-engendered punishment into a spooky circus. The rough-and-ready furnishings at Macbeth's court were gentrified. When Banquo's ghost appears at the feast, Shakespeare's Lady Macbeth mocks her delirious husband by saying 'You look but on a stool'; Davenant more decorously sat the invisible spectre on 'a chair'. The same rudeness had to be expunged from the play's diction, so Davenant changed the adjective in Duncan's abrupt initial question about the Captain who staggers on from the battlefield. 'What bloody man is that?' became 'What agèd man is that?' – more polite, although age would surely have exempted him the fight. The

Garrick declaiming at the 1769 Jubilee in Stratford, with assorted characters from the pageant, engraved by Boydell after Robert Edge Pine.

substitution also snapped the link to Macbeth's later comment on 'the secret'st man of blood', a tortuous phrase that declares his own guilt, even after his wife has washed him clean. Shakespeare's play defines human beings as containers for blood (with an admixture, in Lady Macbeth's case, of gall and milk); Restoration audiences preferred to see man as a citizen, not a wild animal with a troublesome conscience and a talent for poetic speech.

Lennox in Davenant's *Macbeth* reports that 'there is a civil war / Within [the] bosom' of the self-tormented regicide. In 1667 a similar hint about history repeating itself sneaked into *The Tempest, or The Enchanted Island*, a reworking of Shakespeare by Davenant and Dryden. Here Ariel warns Prospero that the quarrelsome castaways have 'parcelled your island into governments' – a reminder of the fractious ideological disputes that followed the execution of Charles I in 1649. The villains Antonio and Alonso now had to make amends for deposing Prospero in Milan, so Davenant and Dryden improbably enlisted them as defenders of the faith: Gonzalo recalls their 'late voyage into Portugal', where they helped repulse 'the Moors of Spain'. To uphold cultural continuity, Shakespeare was awarded regal rank and allied with the Stuart dynasty, which had been welcomed back after the republican experiment failed. The prologue to *The Enchanted Island* honours Shakespeare because 'He, Monarch-like… gave Laws' to Ben Jonson and the other dramatists who followed him – a claim Jonson would have indignantly contested; it goes on to contend that this new play leaves the original intact, which it is bound to do because 'Shakespeare's pow'r is Sacred as a King's'.

In 1681 in *The History of King Lear*, Nahum Tate healed the same political breach by supplying Shakespeare's play with a happy ending. Tate's Cordelia survives to marry Edgar and inherit the throne, while Lear quietly goes off to a 'cool cell' in a hermitage; all that's missing is an eye transplant for Gloster, whose life is also spared. Along with these acts of sentimental clemency, Tate introduced institutional restraints to placate a society still recovering from its recent turmoil. When Goneril and Regan levy new taxes on 'the drudging peasants', they provoke a mutiny, and the House of Commons demands Lear's re-instatement. Defeated by Edgar, the bastard Edmund concedes that 'legitimacy / At last has got it', while Gloster welcomes 'a second birth of empire' and a 'blest restoration'.

Tate viewed *King Lear* as 'a heap of jewels, unstrung and unpolish'd'. In the eighteenth century, Voltaire less generously summed up the plays as an 'enormous dunghill' that contained 'a few pearls'. The baubles did not include *Hamlet*, denounced by Voltaire as a 'barbarous' piece, stuffed with bizarre incidents that would be condemned by 'the vilest public in France or Italy'. The hero, Voltaire pointed out, commits a murder while pretending to kill a rat, and the heroine sings lewd ditties before tumbling into the river, after which a grave is dug on stage and a skull used as a prop during a bout of coarse, silly joking. Alexander Pope commended Shakespeare's originality but still regarded him as a relic of 'Gothick architecture', majestic but overdue for renovation. Policing grammatical faults in his 1725 edition of the plays, Pope tidied up the double superlative in Antony's description of the wound left by Brutus in Caesar's body by changing 'This was the most unkindest cut of all' to 'This, this was the unkindest cut of all'. The alteration, which shifts the emphasis within the phrase, is not an improvement. Pope's stammering repetition gestures towards the physical cut, whereas Shakespeare's over-statement suggestively stresses its symbolic unkindness, its betrayal of kinship, and invokes the fellow-feeling that makes Macbeth reconsider killing Duncan because, as he says, 'I am his kinsman'.

More was at stake here than stylistic correctness: these irregularities seemed like reversions to an unenlightened past. In 1731 Voltaire pitied Shakespeare as an autodidact 'who did not even know Latin' and had the extra misfortune to live 'in a century of ignorance'. The forest of Arden, in this view, was an uncouth lair, fit home for the 'drunken savage' who – Voltaire assumed – had written *Hamlet* while suffering from a hangover.

*

At last in 1765 Samuel Johnson comprehensively pardoned Shakespeare's lapses. The plays, he declared, were a 'map of life', and their conjunctions of tragedy and comedy, which for Voltaire muddled grandeur and grossness, corresponded to the 'chaos of mingled purposes' in human experience. Shakespeare had earned the right to disregard the classical unities and other such arbitrary limits because, Johnson said, he 'engaged… with the world open before him'.

That comment almost paraphrases the conclusion of *Paradise Lost* where, as Adam and Eve depart from Eden, Milton notes that 'The world was all before them' – not an encouraging prospect, because they are about to inaugurate the long penitential trek of human history. But the overcast end of the epic might also serve as the buoyant start of a picaresque novel, where characters leave home, as Shakespeare did, to explore and with luck to conquer the world into which Adam and Eve are unwillingly expelled. Johnson suggested such a connection when he pointed out that Shakespeare's plots were 'generally borrowed from novels', a conveniently eclectic designation that covers a range of ancient and modern narrative sources – Plutarch's political biographies; the chronicles of Holinshed, Geoffrey of Monmouth and Saxo Grammaticus; romances by Ariosto, Spenser and Thomas Lodge; and anthologies of tales like Boccaccio's *Decameron* or Cinthio's *Hecatommithi*, which includes the story of Desdemona and the Moor of Venice and another episode that was adapted in *Measure for Measure*. With hindsight, the term makes Shakespeare the progenitor of a literary form that was new in Johnson's own time.

The early novelists acknowledged the derivation. A literary discussion in Samuel Richardson's *Sir Charles Grandison* contrasts the severe, abstinent Milton with Shakespeare, who thanks to his 'easier, pleasanter, and more intelligible manner of writing' has 'the advantage... in perspicuity', if not in moral seriousness. Shakespeare's lack of a classical education is still a demerit; by way of compensation he is said to be 'an adept in the superior learning, the knowledge of nature'. In *Clarissa*, Richardson's characters cite the plays like secular scripture. Under assault by Lovelace, the chaste heroine quotes Hamlet's attack on the blistered virtue of Gertrude: even though Clarissa is blameless, her self-mortification makes her apply this censure to herself. After raping her, Lovelace calculates that despite her mortification Clarissa will not follow Ophelia's example by committing suicide, and he imagines that Claudio's speech from *Measure for Measure* about the horror of dying might deter her. But Clarissa's version of tragedy goes beyond the sudden, showy climaxes of tragic drama: she succumbs to a protracted, medically undefined malaise, and Richardson's extremely long novel allows her to take her time.

Laurence Sterne reinvented Hamlet as the dithering protagonist of *Tristram Shandy* and revived the decomposed jester Yorick as the sensually susceptible parson who goes travelling in France in *A Sentimental Journey*; in both novels, Shakespeare's tragedy relaxes into a digressive tour of mental foibles and moral frailties. Henry Fielding in *Tom Jones* identifies a Shakespearean source for his average, ordinary hero when Ensign Northerton grumbles about having been made to read Homer, whose name he pronounces 'Homo' – an echo of a comment by Gadshill in *Henry IV*, who says '"homo" is a common name to all men'. Tom Jones is just such an Everyman: novels can do without the self-dramatizing egotists who thrive on stage. The advance from one form to another is confirmed when Tom takes his country-bred servant Partridge to a performance of *Hamlet* with Garrick, who was praised by Johnson for being, like Shakespeare, 'a master in both tragedy and comedy'. Partridge succumbs to gibbering dread when the ghost appears, 'the same passions which succeeded each other in

Hamlet succeeding likewise in him'. But he gives no credit to the actor, since he assumes that the 'little man there upon the stage' is genuinely frightened; he prefers the strutting parodic manner of the oratorical king in the play Hamlet stages. The theatre's feigning defeats itself: why bother artfully imitating life if the mimicry seems so artless?

Garrick decided that no plays would be staged during the Jubilee he organized in Stratford in 1769. Instead he planned a costumed procession of Shakespearean figures – 170 in all, including some noble Romans, Falstaff and his ignoble crew, Anne Boleyn under a canopy for her coronation and Juliet on a bier, plus assorted witches and fairies – who were to file through the town. James Boswell called the *Ode* that Garrick declaimed 'an antique idea, a Grecian thought', because it honoured Shakespeare as 'a mortal transformed into a demi-god, as we read in the pagan mythology'. The notional parade, which in the event was rained off, belonged in the borderless modern world that was to become the novel's domain: having exchanged the stage for the street, the participants could break ranks to tell stories of their own that Shakespeare had not anticipated.

In George Colman's comedy *Man and Wife*, performed later in 1769, the foppish Marcourt arrives in Stratford to attend the Jubilee, and is asked by an acquaintance whether he intends to walk in the pageant 'and show yourself as one of the characters in Shakespeare?' Marcourt, offended by the very thought, says that 'such an original' as himself 'did not exist' in those less florid days. Preposterous as his vanity is, it marks a change in the way the plays were regarded. Shakespeare's self-begotten beings now served as models for those who saw themselves as unrepeatable individuals rather than innocuous, uniform members of the family of man. Hamlet exemplified this new self-consciousness, and Partridge's naïve empathy with him became the obligatory response of more thoughtful Shakespeareans. As the hero of Goethe's novel *Wilhelm Meister's Apprenticeship* prepares to perform the role, he vows to 'pursue [Hamlet] through the strange labyrinths of his caprices and his singularities'. That labyrinth is cranial, like the grey Elsinore of tunnels and twisted staircases in Olivier's film of the play; Wilhelm takes up residence inside the head of the character he adopts as 'my hero'.

The critic A. W. von Schlegel called *Hamlet* 'a tragedy of thought', choosing to ignore Hamlet's spasms of violence and concentrate on his contemplative reveries. 'I have a smack of Hamlet myself, if I may say so', remarked Coleridge, for whom the character's indecision excused his own failure to complete his literary tasks. Hazlitt derived a general rule from that personal declaration. 'It is WE who are Hamlet', he said, since most of us have had some experience of the character's mental blight. As Byron saw it, 'We love Hamlet even as we love ourselves'. Perhaps they all loved Hamlet more than he loved himself: none of them had been ordered by a ghost to kill a king, so they were spared his self-inquisition and self-recrimination. Nor did they have to reckon with the unlovable episodes in which he browbeats Ophelia or slays Polonius. Hazlitt said that Hamlet's predicament, devised by 'the poet's brain', was 'as real as our thoughts'. The mirror was now held up not to all of nature, as Hamlet wished, but to the particular spectator who looked into it, and what it reflected was the mind rather than the face.

This became the preferred way of analysing Shakespeare's characters. In an unapologetically autobiographical study, Hazlitt treated Coriolanus as an artist not a warrior, implicitly goaded by the same triumphant sense of intellectual superiority that produced his own rebarbative essay 'On the Pleasure of Hating'. He explained the appeal of Coriolanus by pointing out that 'The language of poetry naturally falls in with the language of power.' Does that make all poets crypto-fascists? It is a possibility Hazlitt did not investigate, because, separating character from action as romantic critics habitually did, he assumed that the warfare in the play was primarily rhetorical.

Charles Lamb likewise considered Shakespeare's characters to be 'objects of meditation'. On the page Lamb could admire the thrusting spirit and mental intrepidity of Macbeth, Iago or Richard III. On stage, they displeased him by dwindling into criminals. For Coleridge, the jittery, spasmodic acting of Edmund Kean was like 'reading Shakespeare by flashes of lightning'. Theatres had thunder sheets and sizzling flares, but Coleridge's phrase suggests that he would rather have stayed at home and imagined the atmospheric effects. Keats, in his sonnet 'On Sitting Down to Read *King Lear* Once Again', enjoys a painlessly sedentary experience of the play, and savours 'the bitter-sweet of this Shakespearean fruit' as if it were edible – a drama not for cannibals, as Brecht thought, but for epicures with refined tastes.

Richard Wagner – who based his early opera *Das Liebesverbot* on *Measure for Measure*, which he turned into a parable about free love – recited the plays aloud to his family, taking all the parts and transforming the characters into facets of his voluminous ego. He deflected attention from his own philandering by incriminating Desdemona, and told his slavishly devoted wife Cosima that, although she may have done no wrong with Cassio, Othello killed her 'because he knew she must one day be unfaithful to him'. He also used Falstaff as a stand-in for himself, admiring his self-indulgence and his refusal to pay his debts. The appropriation did not end there. In his youth Wagner dreamed that he had met Shakespeare and conversed with him, as equals of course; he once wrote 'To be, or not to be' on a slip of paper and signed his name beneath it, which was tantamount to a claim of authorship.

When the reader replaced the actor, drama narrowed to a dramatic monologue, 'a concert of one' as Henry James called *The Tempest*. Nineteenth-century novelists rescued Shakespeare from this romantic solipsism, propelling his kings and princes into cities where, deprived of their exalted rank, they had to cope with

Henry Wallis, *Shakespeare's House, Stratford-upon-Avon*, c.1854, with mementoes of Hamlet and Macbeth on the stairs.

the same demeaning reality as the rest of us. Tragedy, as James said of George Eliot's *Middlemarch*, was now a consequence of 'unpaid butchers' bills', rather than regicide or royal abdication.

In *Père Goriot*, Balzac replaces the transient hysteria of the stage with a 'living drama acted in silence... on which no curtain is rung down'. Goriot – an impoverished vermicelli seller, left to moulder in a greasy Paris lodging – is a Lear who never had a kingdom. His two upwardly mobile daughters have acquired wealthy husbands, and occasionally visit him to show off their finery; abject rather than enraged, Goriot envies the lapdogs that fawn on them. He lacks a third daughter to stand by him, since bourgeois society produces no selfless, unmercenary Cordelias. The battles in Shakespeare's play may be noises off, but the undeserved misery of Goriot prompts Balzac's go-getting hero Rastignac and his devilish patron Vautrin to instigate a philosophical campaign against property, law and religion. 'It's war between us now!' says Rastignac, shaking his fist at Paris. The orphaned Pip in *Great Expectations* is Dickens's Hamlet, accosted by the grisly convict Magwitch in a graveyard where his parents are buried. Magwitch becomes Pip's ghost, an honorary father but also a benefactor, since instead of demanding revenge he bestows a fortune on the boy and makes possible a London career that brings with it only insecurity and remorse: happy endings, as Pip discovers, can also be tragic. *Crime and Punishment* is Dostoevsky's study of a Macbeth whose crime, the pointless murder of an old pawnbroker, is committed not for self-advancement but to demonstrate his indifference to cowardly morality. In Dostoevsky's *The Possessed*, the young guardsman Stavrogin fights duels, tramples passers-by with his horses, and gleefully insults strangers. His rampages earn him the nickname 'Prince Harry', and his tutor advises his worried mother to read *Henry IV* – but rather than juvenile escapades like Hal's with Falstaff, Stavrogin's outrages are acts of conceptual terror, which eventually include the rape of a child. No timely reformation can be expected: the novel ends with his remorseful suicide.

Aldous Huxley argued that tragic drama tells only a 'partial truth', because the theatre's curtain descends on survivors who are numbed by anguish, unable to look ahead. Novels keep going, as we all must do, recovering from disaster and resuming our lives. Huxley sketched a novelistic extension of *Macbeth*, and imagined Macduff 'eating his supper, growing melancholy, over the whisky, with thoughts of his murdered wife and children, and then, with lashes still wet, dropping off to sleep'. 'Lawful as eating', as Leontes says: the body has its demands, which must be catered to no matter how agonized the mind is.

One novel aims to tell 'the whole truth', as Huxley called it, about an apparently frivolous Shakespearean comedy. Théophile Gautier's *Mademoiselle de Maupin*, published in 1835, uses *As You Like It* as its guide for a riskier journey into the forest and its shady sexual undergrowth. Shakespeare's people only change gender in an emergency – Rosalind, like Viola and Imogen, pretends to be a boy to stay out of danger, and Falstaff dresses up as the fat woman of Brainford so he can escape undetected from Ford's house in *The Merry Wives of Windsor* – and they revert to the correct sex as soon as it is safe to do so. The characters in *Mademoiselle de Maupin* have longings that are more mystically perverse. Chevalier d'Albert envies 'the monstrous bizarre deities of India' with 'their numerous transformations', and itches to know what it felt like for Tiresias to be first male and then female. His friend Théodore, who is Mademoiselle de Maupin in disguise, has already undergone that almost hermaphroditic change, though d'Albert is unaware of it. Performing *As You Like It*, the two of them shed the functional identities imposed by biology and enforced by Christian morality. D'Albert as Orlando deliciously flirts with Théodore as Ganymede, Rosalind's male alias, and is both thrilled and troubled by his infatuation with his fellow actor. A night spent with Maupin resolves d'Albert's uncertainty; relieved to be confirmed as the virile partner, he performs as valiantly as Priapus.

There is, however, an extra complication. D'Albert's mistress Rosette also fancies Théodore, and is unsure whether she wants the object of her desire to be a man or a woman. In the play she is cast as Phebe, the shepherdess who pines for Ganymede but is told she is 'not for all markets'. Gautier refuses to countenance this snobbish rejection: Rosette spends the night with Maupin, and we are left to imagine who did what to whom. *As You Like It* disrupts social conventions but finally upholds them; no hymeneal masque restores conformity in *Mademoiselle de Maupin*. The forest of Arden is now a cushioned boudoir, and the 'country copulatives' mocked by Jaques are refined erotic researchers, more concerned with self-discovery than with reproduction.

*

In 1887 in his *Moralités Légendaires*, Jules Laforgue remarked that Hamlet's thinking was not exhausted by the five acts of Shakespeare's drama. Nor was the range of things that might possibly happen to him. The players Hamlet interviews in Laforgue's sequel are ready to write and perform variants of his already distended personal history: one of them is intriguingly named William, and two others introduce themselves as Ophelia and Kate. With their connivance, Hamlet discovers his true vocation, and resolves to try his luck in the theatre in London, though as he sets out he is slain by Laertes, a social reformer who represents Denmark's future. 'One Hamlet more or less,' Laforgue comments, 'does not mean the end of the human race.'

Other Hamlets were waiting to take over, among them the blocked writer in Iris Murdoch's *The Black Prince*. Shakespeare's play is here interpreted as a parable criticizing the vanity of art, and Murdoch's hero sees the revenger – his own evil genius – as a destructive fantasist who tries to manipulate other people and catastrophically fails. The tragedy is therefore 'a self-castigation in the presence of the god'. God in Borges' fable pardons Shakespeare when he admits that he has fickly migrated between the minds and bodies of others while not knowing who he really is; Murdoch allows Shakespeare to redeem himself in the eyes of a creator who may or may not exist, and on his behalf she frees his characters from the strict control that a play imposes, releasing them into the loose, baggy amplitude of a novel.

John Updike's *Gertrude and Claudius* re-imagines events that occurred before the play begins, and after reconstructing the Danish legend that was Shakespeare's source he contends that nothing much was rotten in Denmark until the malcontent Hamlet returned from university to cause trouble. Updike concludes with the coronation of Claudius, who, having got away with murder, looks ahead in the belief that 'All would be well'. Receding further in time, Ian McEwan's *Nutshell* is a pre-natal prologue to Shakespeare, with Hamlet still snug in the kingdom of infinite space that is the womb. In 'Gertrude Talks Back', a brief confession ghost-written by Margaret Atwood, Hamlet's mother presents her own hard-bitten view of the imbroglio: she denounces her priggish first husband – whom she took the initiative to kill, with no help from Claudius – and blames him for not allowing her to call their son George, which would have spared young Hamlet from having to suffer the porky nicknames his schoolmates pinned on him in the playground.

As these novelists reveal, there is always life after Shakespeare, or before him. Rather than setting an onerous precedent, the plays are an incitement to go further. Falstaff boasts of being 'not only witty in myself, but the cause that wit is in other men', and Shakespeare's creativity has proved equally contagious.

The Forms of Things Unknown

A transparent world
Instrumental language
Storms and serenades
Imaginary work
Picturing metaphors
Painted devils

Defending Shakespeare against his neoclassical detractors, Samuel Johnson insisted that the plays were true to 'the real state of sublunary nature', tethered to 'common life'. That sedate claim had no appeal to romantic enthusiasts, who wanted Shakespeare to be less common, more lunar, perhaps even lunatic.

Lamb, for instance, was glad that Lear's madness kept him 'immethodized from the ordinary purposes of life', free to inveigh against mankind in general during his harangues. In *Mademoiselle de Maupin* Gautier expressed a particular fondness for plays that explored life's 'fascinating strangeness' – notably *A Midsummer Night's Dream* and *The Tempest* with their sprites and imps, their orchestras of insects and disembodied siren songs, controlled in one case by a mischievous hobgoblin, in the other by an angry sorcerer. Thomas De Quincey found an unorthodox cosmology in *The Tempest*, with intimations of 'new modes of life' that were 'preternatural, yet far… from the spiritualities of religion'. He identified the same suspension of 'ordinary life' in *Macbeth* when, after the murder of Duncan, customary reality is 'arrested – laid asleep – tranced – racked into a dread armistice' or 'a deep syncope', only to be startled back into wakeful animation by the knocking at the gate.

Hazlitt accused Johnson of not appreciating 'Shakespeare's bold and happy flights of imagination', which dizzily outstripped language. Johnson, Hazlitt said, undervalued Shakespeare because he lacked the refinement of mind and the passion 'necessary to the painter or musician'. The stipulation is odd, but it reveals that the plays had taken on a more than literary life, spilling over into the other arts.

Pictures and statues in Shakespeare's plays are expected to function as living memories, like the 'counterfeit presentment of two brothers' that Hamlet displays to Gertrude or the replica of Hermione in *The Winter's Tale*, supposedly the work of 'that rare

Italian master, Julio Romano'. But Theseus in *A Midsummer Night's Dream* thinks of art more ambitiously: he tells Hippolyta that 'imagination bodies forth / The forms of things unknown', and later painters strove to do exactly that, turning Shakespearean scenes into metaphysically portentous tableaux, altarpieces for godless romanticism. *Hamlet and Horatio in the Graveyard*, painted by Delacroix in 1835, dressed Hamlet in black, gave him a skull to hold, and placed him, under a sanguine sunset sky, on a diagonally slanted tombstone that looks likely to slide into the crevasse left open by the gravediggers: life is being precipitated into death. This Hamlet makes no jokes about Yorick, and is too wasted by morbidity to challenge Laertes. Lear reminded Lamb of 'Michael Angelo's terrible figures', and when James Barry painted *King Lear Weeping Over the Dead Body of Cordelia* in the late 1780s he gave the now massively strong old man the glowering face of Michelangelo's Moses, together with tempest-tossed white hair and a beard befitting a biblical patriarch. One hand is all that Barry's Lear needs to hold up Cordelia's body, which is as limp as that of Adam on the Sistine Chapel ceiling: in this reversal of Genesis, a sorrowful God finds himself unable to transmit the animating spark to his offspring.

Composers etherealized the plays, hoping to capture what De Quincey, in his characterization of Ariel, called 'a phantom of air'. Music has less exalted uses in Shakespeare's plays, where it is on tap as a household amenity. Orsino hires Feste to sing as mood enhancement, and Bottom, while being entertained by Titania, boasts of possessing 'a reasonable good ear' and calls for 'the tongs and the bones'. The drunken butler Stephano is pleased by the instrumental twangling that resonates on Prospero's island, because it means that when he becomes governor 'I shall have my music for nothing'. Sometimes music's uses are uglier: Iago stirs up a riot with the help of a drinking song he says he learned in England.

Romanticism rescued art from all such invidious chores. Victor Hugo called Shakespeare a force of nature, 'a vast wind blowing off the shores of a world'. Musicians made this elemental energy audible, and painters, infatuated with Shakespearean ghosts and gambolling fairies, replaced characters who were merely human with an otherworldly cast of riders on that poetic cyclone.

*

At the end of *Love's Labour's Lost*, the chirping of the cuckoo gives way to the tuneless nocturnal screeching of an owl, and a wintry coughing epidemic in church overwhelms the parson's sermon. 'The words of Mercury', as Armado says, 'are harsh after the songs of Apollo.' Shakespeare often leaves us with such unmelodious harshness: Lear's reiterated 'Never', Macbeth's 'Hold, enough!' Midnight clangs with an 'iron tongue' to conclude *A Midsummer Night's Dream*, and Fortinbras orders a peal of ordnance that will silence any mutterings about the fate of Denmark after Hamlet's death. Music, by contrast, filters down from sunny Apollo's domain, where light is sound – a region more perfect than that of drama.

Henry Purcell's *The Fairy Queen*, first performed in 1692, begins this lyrical amelioration of Shakespeare. It is not quite an operatic version of *A Midsummer Night's Dream*, because the uncredited adaptation of Shakespeare that it uses is a garbled mess; Purcell set none of Shakespeare's words, instead scoring a series of masques that are laid on as royal entertainments, to divert Titania or to celebrate Oberon's birthday. Music tames the comedy, civilizing Shakespeare as Restoration taste required. The seasons – distempered or hybridized in the play because of the quarrel that divides the fairy kingdom – line up again in their proper sequence when a chorus hails nature, 'Great Parent of us

Hamlet and Horatio at the Cemetery by Delacroix, 1839
– a different version of a scene that Delacroix previously
painted in 1835.

all'. A 'Peaceful Train' of attendants sings Titania blissfully to sleep without requiring her or any of the other characters to writhe through delirious nightmares, while a counter-tenor seductively insinuates that 'One charming night / Brings more delight / Than a hundred happy days' – not a judgement with which Shakespeare's frazzled lovers would probably agree. Purcell's Oberon, who is more a theatrical impresario than a noctambulant demon king, commands 'Let a new Transparent World be seen', and the machinery of the Restoration stage was able to execute the order: arbours parted to reveal a grotto, fountains spouted real water, swans cruised on a stream bridged by the bodies of dragons, monkeys did a jig, and exotic birds fluttered in an entirely extraneous Chinese garden.

Felix Mendelssohn's overture to the *Dream*, first performed in 1826, had no need of such elfin engineering: it concentrates on atmosphere, dispensing with both scenery and language. Music, like magic, restages the action in immaterial air. The bothersome preliminaries at the Athenian court are brushed aside, and an aural spell produces instant enchantment. Four drowsy, harmonically blurred chords sound on the woodwinds, as if exhaled by the moonlit forest. They hang suspended, almost visibly aglow, punctuated by tantalizing silences, after which the different worlds juggled by the play start into life and chase each other through dimensionless musical space. Soft staccato figurations on the violins represent the fairies, the officious pomp of the full orchestra introduces the law-giving Duke. There are impassioned lyrical outbursts by the lovers, rustic drones to announce the rude mechanicals, and a braying tuba for Bottom's transmogrification. Horns accompany Theseus and his hunters. In 1843 Mendelssohn returned to the play and contributed incidental music to a performance in Potsdam, underscoring some of the speeches – but everything essential is distilled in the overture, with not a word spoken.

Dryden called Shakespeare a king; Hector Berlioz prayerfully addressed him as God the Father and made him an elective parent, the source of his own musical creativity. As Shakespeare's offspring, Berlioz was almost physically affiliated with a variety of possible siblings, and he juggled alter egos that he extracted from his favourite plays. The narrator of *Lélio, ou Le Retour à la vie* – a monodrama or 'méloloque' appended to his autobiographical *Symphonie fantastique* – starts as Hamlet and ends as Prospero. Awakening from the symphony's bad dream, Lélio remembers having written a suicide note to his friend Horatio. Did he die and has he now recovered, or is he perhaps in purgatory, like the ghost of Hamlet's father? He reconsiders Hamlet's surmises about the afterlife, and is haunted by an unseen orchestra and a keening choir. Then, regaining his self-control, he adopts the alternative persona and organizes some attendant spirits to perform his musical fantasia on *The Tempest*, which urges Miranda to quit her illusory island and sail home to sunny Italian reality. When Lélio slumps in Hamlet-like melancholy and listens to voices in his head, music is neurosis; when he takes up a baton that is his equivalent to Prospero's staff, it becomes self-prescribed therapy. Shakespeare both infects Berlioz with the romantic disease and supplies him with the classical cure.

The Shakespearean music of Berlioz digressively opens out the plays. In his *Tristia* a chorus follows Ophelia as she drifts downstream, intoning a text by Ernest Legouvé that lyrically grieves over her 'douce et tendre folie'; a funeral march for Hamlet ensues, with the chorus now emitting wordless cries of grief or terror that Fortinbras, who takes charge of the obsequies in the play, would surely not have permitted. In *Béatrice et Bénédict*, an opera that eccentrically adapts *Much Ado About Nothing*, Berlioz sends Hero and her maid Ursula on an extra-Shakespearean detour into the nocturnal garden, where they sing about a happiness that paradoxically saddens them. After they stroll out of sight – which is when the dramatic scene, if it existed in *Much Ado About Nothing*, would have had to end – the orchestra listens to the gathering darkness for two rapt minutes. Leaves rustle, water softly splashes, birds settle in the trees, and a scarcely audible pulsation might be the earth adjusting its internal rhythms as it falls asleep. Tragically or comically, music subjugates Shakespeare's language – in *Tristia* first allowing it to be drowned, then forcing it to stare open-mouthed at nothingness; in *Béatrice et Bénédict* letting it lapse into a brief pastoral symphony.

A similar expansion of Shakespeare's poetry occurs in Berlioz's operatic epic *Les Troyens*, during a swooning love duet in which Virgil's Dido and Aeneas borrow some lines from *The Merchant of Venice*. Their source is a flippant, sophistical dialogue between Lorenzo and Jessica, who accuse each other of infidelity by citing ancient precursors for their own shaky relationship: on just such a balmy night Troilus sighed for the treacherous Cressida, Thisbe arrived for her rendezvous with Pyramus (which ended badly, as we know from *A Midsummer Night's Dream*), and the bereft Dido waved to Aeneas as he vanished on the horizon. Lorenzo and Jessica are retelling stories whose meaning they twist to suit themselves; the Didon and Enée of Berlioz belong in that world of classical myth, since he is the son of Venus, and rather than joking about their own imperfection they describe the loves of the gods with a knowing sensuality that is intensified by the musical atmosphere – a sultry Carthaginian night, a lapping sea, a fanning breeze, all evoked by the respiration of the drowsy, murmuring orchestra and by voices afloat on a divan of languorous air. With only words to describe Portia's moonlit garden at Belmont, Shakespeare's stage for once seems almost bare and arid by comparison.

Berlioz heard in the first movement of Beethoven's Fifth Symphony the emotional turbulence of 'a great soul fallen prey to despair', and was reminded of the scene in the third act of *Othello* when the hero, tortured by Iago, lunges between psychotic fury and tender regret. In his review of a concert he printed excerpts from the play beneath motifs from the symphony, as if Beethoven had composed a wordless monologue for the distraught character. Shakespeare and Beethoven, Berlioz concluded, both plumbed the depths of the human heart, though they did so by different means; in his *Roméo et Juliette* he dialectically merged them, folding a Shakespearean drama into a choral symphony modelled on Beethoven. The dramatic symphony, as Berlioz called it, begins with a contralto who rhapsodizes about the bliss of first love under an Italian sky and worshipfully praises 'notre divin Shakespeare', and it ends as Père Laurence, in the service of a more official divinity, takes over from the bass who suppresses growling disorder in Beethoven's Ninth Symphony and prevails on the antagonistic Montagues and Capulets to make peace. Berlioz grants Mercutio a vocal solo, because for the romantics his homage to Mab and her magic described the skittish workings of Shakespeare's mind. But Romeo and Juliet remain in the orchestra, speaking what Berlioz called an 'instrumental language, which is richer, more varied, less finite' – horn and cello for him, oboe and flute for her.

In Tchaikovsky's 'fantasy-overture' to *Romeo and Juliet*, that instrumental language confides the composer's own sexual secrets. Re-imagining the play as a plaintive autobiography, Tchaikovsky excludes the flippancy of Mercutio and the seasoned wisdom of Juliet's Nurse; instead he sharpens the showdown between the clashing swords of the inimical families and the aching ardour of the lovers. The music first emerges from the pious gloom where Friar Laurence hovers: desire is here menaced by religion as much as by a familial feud. Whereas Shakespeare's Romeo and Juliet die by accident, Tchaikovsky's pair nurture a forbidden love that can only find consummation in a suicide pact.

Richard Strauss attempted a similar compression of drama in

his symphonic poem *Macbeth*. In the play, Macbeth says that 'sound and fury' signify nothing; for Strauss, however, they dramatize the brazen din of war and the surreptitious violence of murder. The youthful Strauss was proud of the score's avant-garde discordance – an iron-clad militaristic ferocity when Macbeth strides on, acid alarums from the wind instruments that sound like Lady Macbeth's hoarse raven – just as Verdi, when preparing his opera *Macbeth* in 1847, said only half jokingly that he wanted a soprano who would croak out Lady Macbeth's imprecations with a rough, hollow voice instead of euphoniously singing an aria.

With Shakespeare's encouragement, music advanced beyond its traditional mission of making conflict and discord 'tunable'. Theseus uses that word in *A Midsummer Night's Dream* when he tells Hippolyta that his baying hounds are 'matched in mouth like bells, / Each under each', so that they yap and bark in octaves. Given this preference for sounds that placate the ear, it's not surprising that, when choosing entertainments for his wedding feast, he rejects the offer of a play that will represent 'The riot of the tipsy Bacchanals, / Tearing the Thracian singer in their rage'. That summary anticipates the mythological programme of romantic music, which denied a monopoly to Apollo: the Thracian singer Orpheus is slain by the besotted female followers of Dionysus, whose orgiastic triumph has an echo in many symphonic and operatic versions of Shakespeare's tragedies.

Verdi's *Otello* – first performed, like Strauss's *Macbeth*, in 1887 – starts with something like the 'fracas sublime' that galvanized Berlioz at the first Shakespeare performance he attended. The play opens with a bantering conversation in a Venetian street; the opera begins among a panicking mob on the quay in Cyprus during a hurricane, and instantly whips up perhaps the loudest, most stunning onslaught of tuned noise ever heard in a theatre. A thunderclap rumbles on the bass drum, a gong and cymbals simulate a lightning strike, an organ with its stops open makes the walls shudder and the floor quake; jagged volleys of brass suggest that this may be the ultimate day of wrath. The chorus cries out in dread, buffeted by rhythmic surges. Once the uproar abates, Verdi endeavours to duplicate in music the linguistic extremities of Shakespearean drama. The operatic Desdemona sings with angelic serenity; the beauty of the sound she makes confers on her a kind of beatitude, and all traces of the earthy wit and stubborn will she displays in Shakespeare are smoothed away. Lyricism is her personal prerogative, denied to the other characters. Otello rants, shouts, and stops singing altogether when he is toppled, gasping, by an epileptic fit. Iago, according to Verdi's instructions, chatters seditiously or snarls and guffaws, always too disruptive and ironic to sustain a melody.

On Shakespeare's stage, only one person speaks at a time. At points of crisis Verdi extends the range of drama by allowing everyone to sing, but not in unison. In his vast synchronized ensembles, different reactions entwine and overlap, and we seem able to overhear them all – an ultra-Shakespearean aural skill, which recognizes that every individual has a point of view and a right to express it. The spoiled banquet in Verdi's *Macbeth* concludes in a communal stocktaking. In the play, Lady Macbeth covers her embarrassment by bossily dismissing the guests: 'Stand not upon the order of your going,' she says, 'but go at once'. Verdi keeps everyone on stage for five immobile minutes, during which Macbeth ponders the ghost's appearance and makes plans to consult the witches, Lady Macbeth derides his feebleness, Macduff resolves to escape across the border, and the courtiers bemoan their subjection to a mad king. In *Otello*, when the rabid Moor strikes Desdemona in front of the Venetian ambassador, music universalizes the incident. She grieves and is comforted by Emilia, he continues to rail, Iago mutters as he adjusts his plot to take account of Cassio's sudden promotion, Lodovico is scandalized, and the chorus gives vent to shock and perplexity; gradually

Desdemona's voice rises above all the others in a lament that despite her agony diffuses forgiveness. Her first words are 'A terra!', since she has been knocked to the floor, but by the time Otello interrupts the ensemble seven minutes later, she is vocally ascendant.

Falstaff, Verdi's valedictory opera, ends in Windsor forest as all the characters – whether gloating like the merry wives or humbled like their male dupes – agree not to bear grudges and join in a rollicking fugue that declares life to be a joke. Instead of the divergent pleas and rankling disputes amassed in *Otello*, here there is consensus. The pace quickens, sparking off a fusillade of high notes and an eruption of rhythmic laughter; we feel the globe rotate like a spinning top, revved up by the spirit of comedy. Words alone, even if they are Shakespeare's, can hardly induce such exhilaration.

In his recitation at the Jubilee, Garrick hailed Falstaff as 'a comic world in ONE!', a 'huge, misshapen heap' replete with wit, fancy, humour, whim and jest. This orotund, one-man world threatens to take over the plays in which he appears, and Shakespeare had to put him on the defensive: he is marginalized and then banished in *Henry IV*, satirically demeaned in *The Merry Wives of Windsor*, and in *Henry V* he dies offstage. In 1913 Elgar's *Falstaff* made him at last the uncontested hero of a 'symphonic study' that could also be called a musical novel. Elgar disagreed with Johnson's stern moral critique of the character, preferring to trust a tendentious essay written in 1777 by Maurice Morgann, who described Falstaff as a respectable cavalier, a valiant soldier and an appropriate companion for a prince. Elgar also cited with approval Ernest Dowden's claim that Falstaff is as complex as Hamlet – equally slippery and erratic, and increasingly prone to depression. A tone poem spares us the sight of Falstaff's sweating bulk, and has no use for his witty verbal ingenuity. Elgar's score briefly sketches Falstaff's carousing in the tavern, the shambles of his recruiting drive and his flustered ride to Hal's coronation, but his music deals in emotion not action, and it turns Falstaff inside out by prolonging his sad reverie about his limber adolescence as a page and sympathizing with his mood of autumnal melancholy. The orchestral traversal of what Elgar called 'the whole of human life' – which he said was Shakespeare's true subject in the history plays – concludes with a harrowing transcription of Falstaff's death, during which thematic wisps from his past flutter through his head before consciousness fades. In *Henry V* we have to rely on Mistress Quickly's blundering reminiscence; Elgar gives us a direct experience of the body's enfeeblement and the mind's unravelling.

In *The Merchant of Venice*, after the exchange with Jessica from which Berlioz borrowed in *Les Troyens*, Lorenzo delivers a lecture on the music of the spheres. He is sceptical about the power of Orpheus to move rocks and trees, and says that 'the poet / Did feign' when describing such feats, but he values the 'sweet sounds' as a means of social and moral control. Music, Lorenzo believes, can calm 'wild and wanton' animals and appease those who are 'hard, and full of rage'. At this point in the play it is a contentious assertion: no such lyrical intercession soothed Shylock or his tormenters. In 1938 in his *Serenade to Music* Ralph Vaughan Williams shared out this speech among sixteen favourite vocal soloists, with a lark-like violin and plucked harps to waft the voices and trumpet calls to rally them. In the play Jessica listens meekly to Lorenzo, and is given only one line halfway through his speech. 'I am never merry when I hear sweet music', she says, which either implies discreet disagreement or conveys her uneasy emotional state. Vaughan Williams makes restitution for her silence by awarding the headiest climaxes to his eight sopranos, while the male soloists mutter ominously about the discontent of those whose souls are unmusical. Abstracted from drama by the *Serenade*, Lorenzo's starchy discourse is sublimated.

'How comes this gentle concord in the world?' asks the Duke at the end of *A Midsummer Night's Dream*, surprised by the reconciliation of the warring lovers. For him as for Lorenzo, music is a peacekeeping agent. This benediction was challenged by modern composers, who often found in Shakespeare's plays a pretext for what Arnold Schoenberg called 'the emancipation of dissonance'. After his experiment with sonic belligerence in *Macbeth*, in 1918 Strauss composed a set of lieder based on Ophelia's mad songs – snatches of crazed, indecent thinking with intermittent funereal moans, delivered in a dizzy vocal gabble that is seconded by atonal skips and leaps on the piano.

When Jean Sibelius provided a score for a Copenhagen production of *The Tempest* in 1925, he started with an overture that inundates Shakespeare's words: the opening scene on the stricken ship was omitted, because the stage could hardly compete with the tumult already heard from the orchestra. Wind howls, and seasick rhythms lurch and heave; the sound circles as if in a maelstrom. A lumbering tune Sibelius wrote for Caliban re-establishes solidity, although the harmonium and harp, associated with Miranda and Ariel, aerate the texture all over again. Towards the end, when Iris presides over the harvest festival, Sibelius composed the sonic equivalent to a rainbow – a hazy, humming spectrum of notes that suggests iridescence. Sun and moon, however, remain at odds: for Prospero's renunciation of magic, the stage director requested 'lunatic music', as if remembering the equation Theseus makes between lunacy and poetry, and Sibelius obliged with a spasm of thundery violence, in which the orchestra rumbles and sometimes shrieks. The elemental din has flared up again inside Prospero's unharmonized head.

Other cataclysms followed, as music marched Shakespeare through the fraught history of the twentieth century. In Sergei Prokofiev's ballet *Romeo and Juliet*, composed while he was being bullied by the Stalin's cultural commissars in Russia during the

1930s, the Duke puts an end to the street brawl between Montagues and Capulets with a terrifying sonic gesture – an orchestral crash that has the force of a blow to the brain, with a shrill high-pitched scream of protest slicing through the concussion as it spreads to take up all aural space. A military band struts offstage during an orchestral interlude, erecting a barricade of impenetrable brass; ready for deployment, the knights at the Capulet ball lumpenly dance in their chainmail. The envious tiff between rival families here matters less than a totalitarian regime that crushes individual freedom when the Duke bangs his adamantine fist. In Aribert Reimann's opera *Lear*, first performed in Munich in 1978, the division of the kingdom – announced immediately by Lear on one doggedly repeated note, before the orchestra's entry – summarizes the modern schisms of a divided continent. Extra contingents of brass and percussion bray and clatter in a churning cacophony. What Reimann calls 'neurotic writing on the high woodwind' catches the keening malice of Goneril and Regan, while the Fool's ditties are accompanied by a string quartet – the ensemble of co-operative classical rationality, here dedicated to the praise of folly. On the heath, an agglomerated chord vibrates as if from beneath the floor, seismically.

Caliban first says that 'the isle is full of noises', and although he adds that those 'sounds and sweet airs… hurt not', his qualification does not apply to the brutalism of Prokofiev's Duke, or to the pandemonium of Reimann's storm. Lorenzo's speech about the music of the spheres refers to men with 'affections dark as Erebus', who are 'fit for treasons, stratagems and spoils'; deafened by the 'muddy vesture of decay', they are unable to hear the choiring orbs above. The shadowy lowland where they live is the terrain of drama, peopled by Shakespearean characters who speak in verse but do not always know how to sing.

*

During the heroine's perusal of the Trojan painting in *The Rape of Lucrece*, Shakespeare comments that 'In scorn of nature, art gave lifeless life'. Forms that are still and silent seem able to move and speak: the dry eyes of dead Trojans look tearful, and Nestor's beard wags while 'from his lips did fly / Thin winding breath' that sculpts his 'golden words'. 'Much imaginary work was there,' Shakespeare concludes, and some of it has to be done by viewers, who complete the artist's 'conceit deceitful' by picturing what 'was left unseen, save to the eye of mind'. This was the challenge confronted by painters who illustrated Shakespeare's plays. How would their wordless art measure up to the vivacity of his language? And could they see around corners, depicting scenes he missed out?

At first, artists were content to supply souvenirs of actual performances. A 1709 engraving shows Thomas Betterton as Hamlet with his father's ghost in Gertrude's closet. Hamlet has a luxuriant periwig, the ghost clanks in full armour, and Gertrude remains seated, regally composed. All three semaphore mild surprise by holding up their hands; a chair reacts somewhat more dramatically by tumbling over. Painted in 1745 by William Hogarth, Garrick's Richard III recoils in alarm from the ghosts of his victims. With a curtained tent on the battlefield as his small portable theatre, the actor assumes a celebrated pose and waits to have it eternalized. In 1768 Johann Zoffany painted Garrick and his colleague Mrs Pritchard after the murder of Duncan: dressed in eighteenth-century formal attire, they look as if an arresting officer has caught them gorily red-handed and told them to freeze. Acting – at least until Kean's more energetic Shakespearean performances laid bare what Hazlitt called the 'whirlwind of the soul' – consisted of striking attitudes, which suited the static art of portraiture.

J. M. W. Turner in his Shakespearean paintings ignored the theatre's constraints and allowed characters to roam outside and lose themselves in an urban crush. *A Street in Venice*, to which Turner attached a terse quotation from an exchange between Shylock and Antonio, is about the clogged alleys that spill into the Grand Canal, the people jostling on jetties or balanced insecurely on gondolas, the birds diving for scraps, and the flood of sunlight that almost liquefies whatever remains solid in the amphibious city. An effort is required to spot the saturnine man with the sharpened dagger, who in any case ought to be indoors at the court hearing. Turner's *Jessica* was exhibited with a jumbled quotation from Shylock, who tells his daughter to close the windows of his house. The painting celebrates her disobedience in another tribute to dazing light: she resembles an aureole, burning through the shuttered gloom that Shylock demands. *Juliet and Her Nurse* transplants Shakespeare's characters from Verona to Venice, where they allow Turner to depict the Piazza San Marco under a sky set ablaze by fireworks, with tidal crowds awash in the square below the balcony on which the two women perch. A sky alight, a flood – the scene could have been as disastrous as Colman's *Edge of Doom*. Instead Turner offers a kind of salvation, opening out the claustrophobia of tragedy: this pyrotechnical festivity subsumes or submerges the plight of individuals.

In *Queen Mab's Cave* Turner painted a place that for Mercutio is purely imaginary, the cranial recess in which dreams are incubated by Mab, 'the fairies' midwife'. Mercutio assumes that Mab goes to work overnight; Turner painted her headquarters in blazing daylight, and did not confine her activity to the minds of sleepers like Romeo. Set in an aqueous landscape suffused by a glowing mist, with mermaids swimming, swans taking flight and a honey-coloured castle that wavers in the air, the cave glows like a furnace. The secret den that houses Shakespeare's imagination has the kinetic heat of a factory.

Mercutio's metaphors exist in an indistinct zone that is hard to visualize, as he acknowledges. Mab's coach gouged from a

overleaf
Juliet and Her Nurse by J. M. W. Turner, 1836.

hazelnut, the gnat that drives it and the saddled atoms that draw it – these, he admits, are all the 'children of an idle brain, / Begot of nothing but vain fantasy'. William Blake ignored Mercutio's flippant disavowal and set out to make images of such gauzy similes – for instance, the personification of Pity that Macbeth envisages as

> a naked new-born babe,
> Striding the blast, or heaven's cherubim, horsed
> Upon the sightless couriers of the air.

Macbeth's words are contradictory but revealingly so, like the incoherent narratives unpicked by the analysts of dreams. Can an infant stride, and do so while upright on a gale? No sooner have we tried to visualize this than the baby mutates into a winged angel, with the baffling proviso that the horse the cherub is riding may not actually be there. This clash between childlike fragility and heroic potency catches Macbeth's own combination of physical strength and emotional or moral weakness; it also hints at his self-pitying anxiety about his lack of heirs, which makes him want to eliminate the offspring of Banquo and Macduff. 'Sightless' might mean invisible or blind or both: whichever it is, the word defies us to picture what it describes, just as it spares Macbeth from having to look at the evidence of his misdeeds. But in Blake's design, Macbeth disappears, as does the dramatic situation. Instead the equestrian cherub removes Pity from a recumbent, possibly dead mother just after delivery, intending to spirit the infant away from the downtrodden human world. The rescue is necessary because, as Blake put it in his poem 'The Human Abstract', 'Pity would be no more, / If we did not make somebody Poor': the facile compassion we expend on others simply makes us feel better about social inequalities, as we do after giving alms to a beggar. Macbeth's psychologically candid muddle becomes an allegory extracted from Blake's personal theological system.

previous page
Queen Mab's Cave by J. M. W. Turner, 1846.

In 'As if an Angel dropp'd down from the Clouds', Blake metamorphoses another Shakespearean metaphor. The title comes from Vernon's account of Prince Hal armed and mounted for battle; it is meant to prod Hotspur into reacting furiously, which it does. With the speech as his excuse, Blake again independently elaborates a myth of his own. A seraph, naked rather than armour-clad, drops literally from a cloud, but not, as in Vernon's account, to ride a 'fiery Pegasus' and 'witch the world with noble horsemanship'. Instead the enormous stallion leaps up to meet him; its hooves rebound from a sliver of rock as it takes flight, while a rising sun announces a new dispensation in the universe. The barren rock represents what Blake thought of as sterile Newtonian reason, and the horse might be the airborne creative mastery of Shakespeare, a reproof to the mundane scientific intellect. We are a long way from the military manoeuvres in *Henry IV*.

Lady Macbeth ridicules her husband for being childishly afraid of a 'painted devil'. 'The sleeping and the dead', she says, 'are but as pictures', which renders them harmless. It is an enviably cold-blooded theory: in fact demonic images – like the elves and goblins from *A Midsummer Night's Dream* painted by Joseph Noël Paton, with a malign, pointy-eared Puck as their giant overseer – are fetishes designed to fix fear, like a face on a leering tribal mask, and with luck cast it out. In *Lady Macbeth Seizing the Daggers*, exhibited in 1812, Henry Fuseli's Macbeth stands paralysed by dread in the doorway of the room where he has done the killing; his wife – enormously muscular, her dress billowing, her hair looped and piled up in a domineering crown – swoops towards him to take control, with a finger on her lips to enjoin silence. Her gesture is an embargo on telling our dreams, a taboo challenged by Fuseli when he painted this black and poisonously grey-green nightmare. In Fuseli's *Macbeth, Banquo and the Witches*, painted in 1793–4, Macbeth grips his sword as if it could defend him

overleaf
Pity by Blake, c.1795.

overleaf
Puck and Fairies by Joseph Noel Paton, c.1850.

against those vaporous fortune-tellers, who tantalized illustrators because they ought to be unpaintable: when questioned, they slip out of their bodies 'Into the air, and what seemed corporal / Melted, as breath into the wind'.

John Martin's version of Macbeth's encounter with the witches, which dates from about 1820, makes the tiny Shakespearean characters almost incidental to a geological and meteorological convulsion far exceeding the murky weather at the start of the play. Mountain ranges that jut out of the quaking earth are lashed by an intemperate sky, in which clouds sharpen into points like scythes; an ant-like army in the valley awaits the apocalypse. The witches are housed in a metaphor: Banquo says 'The earth hath bubbles, as the water has', and here a thin transparent membrane encloses the three women, who despite the fragility of their container are near-naked giantesses, not wrinkled hags. A ray deriving from some remote point in the sky strikes a spark beneath their aerial vehicle, indicating that they are revenants from another world. Macbeth, not merely taken aback as in the play, may be contemplating a suicidal leap from that jagged crag: sublime terror has tipped over into extraterrestrial horror.

Romantic artists set themselves to compete with Shakespeare's most illusory poetry. Their Victorian successors chose to ground the plays in history, a tendency anticipated by Martin's decision to dress Macbeth and Banquo in tartans; alternatively the characters were earthed, implanted in nature. John Everett Millais posed the model for his *Ophelia* in a bathtub in his studio, with oil lamps to keep the water warm, then travelled to the Hogsmill River in suburban London to paint the stream and its mossy, overgrown bank. He even added a water vole, which paddled beside Ophelia until he was persuaded to cover it over. When the picture was exhibited in 1852, a botany professor assembled his pupils in front of it and, ignoring the sodden, insane suicide that it portrays,

previous page
Ophelia by John Everett Millais, 1851–2.

lectured them on the vegetation. In Shakespeare's play, the language of the flowers, which are genitalia, is subtly inflammatory. The wild orchids or long purples in Ophelia's bouquet are not meant to display the entangled variety of the countryside, which is how the earnest botanist saw them; as Gertrude implies by alluding to their 'grosser' nickname when she describes the scene, they convey the illicit thoughts of women who cannot speak directly about desire and fertility. Both in the studio and on location, the realism that Millais strove for disrupted the surreal scene he had chosen to paint. The model for Ophelia caught a cold when the bath water cooled, and Millais suffered his own 'martyrdom', as he called it, when he was stung by the flies that swarmed on the riverbank.

He struggled harder to hold together nature and the supernatural, the visual and the visionary, when he painted Ferdinand being led astray by the bodiless Ariel's song in *The Tempest*. 'Where should this music be?' asks Ferdinand: Millais could not avoid answering the question, although by making the sprite visible he risked demystifying the encounter. In an additional complication, the song's report on the death of Ferdinand's father is a lie. Millais has Ariel whisper the information in confidence to the young man, who strains to understand; a sour-faced bat stops its ears as if wishing to hear no evil, while another of Ariel's familiars closes its puckered mouth with its fingers – the same cautionary gesture used by Fuseli's Lady Macbeth, though here it signals a determination to speak no evil, rather than enjoining silence as a cover for crime. Why the embarrassment? Poetic metaphors take permissible liberties with the facts, as Ariel does in his song when he turns Alonso's bones into coral, his eyes into pearls. Millais, however, followed the gospel of John Ruskin, who instructed painters to study nature, 'believing all things to be right and good and rejoicing always in the truth'. He therefore began by painting the microscopically

overleaf
Macbeth, Banquo and the Three Witches by John Martin, *c.*1820.

Ferdinand Lured by Ariel by John Everett Millais, 1849–50.

accurate background in a field outside Oxford and wished that he could have spent a month on every weed, perhaps because that would that have delayed having to reckon with the fantasy and falsehood of the dramatic episode that he superimposed on the landscape. Although he thought better of the water rat in *Ophelia*, here he included some fugitive lizards in the grass at Ferdinand's feet: Ariel's bright green body could be explained away as adaptive camouflage, like the skin of the little reptiles. When Ferdinand was added, the wrinkles around the knee of his fifteenth-century Italian tights poked out almost three-dimensionally, so that he seems to be stepping forward to find a way out of the painting – an escape from both the poet's lyrical fiction and the painter's moral myopia.

Modernism abandoned Ruskin's respect for healthy open-air reality, and freed illustrators to picture scenes that are deliberately obscured by Shakespeare. Macduff, emerging from the room in which Duncan lies dead, dares the lookers-on to cross that border: 'Approach the chamber, and destroy your sight', he says, warning that 'a new Gorgon' awaits within. Here is the tragedy's blind spot, denied to our eyes but accessible to unbridled imagination. The Russian director Sergei Eisenstein obsessively choreographed the carnage inside that room in a series of drawings made in 1931. In one of these, Macbeth and his wife nakedly copulate on the floor beneath the king's strung-up corpse, which has been both decapitated and flayed; in other versions, Duncan is quartered by Lady Macbeth's carving knife, or slit open vertically in a surgical incision that exposes his heart, lungs and intestines. These were Eisenstein's gruesomely perverse conjectures, though they also refer to the torments to which Picasso's cubism subjected the human form: man is now a piece of work of a very different kind, only too easily dismantled.

Salvador Dalí, who illustrated *Macbeth* for an edition published in 1946, used Duncan's drunken guards – their heads lolling, their swords slipping out of their hands – as symbols of the mind with its defences lowered. Dalí drew Duncan's horses eating each other, one of the unimaginable portents mentioned by Ross in the play, and he made the soldiers who strap boughs from Birnam wood on to their backs look like hybrid creatures, a miscegenation of animal and vegetable. His witches brew their potion in an obscene laboratory that no set designer could ever construct. An octopus with a woman's head fastens its suckers on a gutted minotaur, its spare arms clasping crucibles in which human body parts are mashed and blended; its skull splits open to allow for a brain transplant, and a bent fork and a twisted ladle show, as Dalí so often does, that matter is putrid, decadent, never remaining firm and stable for long. Dalí's schizoid Lady Macbeth has a bifurcated head, with two eyes that roll inwards to stare at each other and a pair of mouths that utter contradictory messages. Here we can glimpse the multiple personalities that inhabit a single Shakespearean character and, according to Borges, fought it out inside Shakespeare himself.

Likewise in Edward Gordon Craig's woodcut *Hamlet and Daemon*, made in 1909 during his work on a Moscow production of the play, a supplementary head that belongs to a morbid spirit-companion nestles on the frowning prince's shoulder and whispers in his ear like the Ariel of Millais, drawing him towards death. In the closet scene, Gertrude asks Hamlet why 'you do bend your eye on vacancy / And with th' incorporal air do hold discourse?' Puzzled by his hallucinating, she adds 'all that is I see'. What she misses is the ghost, or the bogey into which Gordon Craig transformed it. For her the phantom, as she says, remains a 'bodiless creation' that must be 'the very coinage of [Hamlet's] brain'. Despite her disbelief, this defines the purpose of Shakespeare illustration at its boldest: it makes visible what we cannot see.

Hamlet with his shadow self by E. G. Craig.

All Which It Inherit

Pride and glory
After the empire
Lear on the steppes and in the outback
Shaking Mr Shakespeare
We shadows

'Triumph, my Britain,' urged Ben Jonson, who expected 'all Scenes of Europe' to pay homage to the country graced by Shakespeare's birth. Adding an edge of aggression to the boast, Garrick's *Ode* likened Shakespeare's pen to Alexander the Great's conquistadorial sword. Lovelace in *Clarissa* – a litterateur as well as a libertine – hails Shakespeare as 'our English pride and glory', a phrase that further extends Jonson's exhortation. Pride implies power, and glory, its adjunct in the Lord's Prayer, is an attribute of kingship and of national or imperial pre-eminence: did Shakespeare matter because he vouched for Britain's greatness?

This patriotic ardour masked a cosier complacency. In a portrait by Gainsborough, Garrick leans against a bust of Shakespeare that has been pastorally positioned under a tree in an aristocrat's park. Garrick's arm wraps round the sculpture's plinth; his head almost nestles on its stony shoulder. The stance is casually proprietorial, taking Shakespeare for granted because he has always been there, vegetating in the shrubbery while ivy clambers up his pedestal. Garrick perhaps had reason for treating him with such familiarity: the dramatist's survival depends on the actor. Without having striven to keep Shakespeare alive, others were pleased that he gave them an unearned advantage in the world. 'We all talk Shakespeare,' says Edmund Bertram in Jane Austen's *Mansfield Park*, as if remembering the earnest commonplaces that Polonius or the Countess in *All's Well That Ends Well* recite to their departing sons. The dilettantish Henry Crawford agrees, despite not having opened a volume of the plays since leaving school. 'Shakespeare one gets acquainted with without knowing how,' he says. 'It is a part of an Englishman's constitution.' Heritage is genetic, which spares him from having to do his homework.

Less lazily, Coleridge declared that the history plays were written 'to make Englishmen proud of being Englishmen', and in a lecture delivered in 1813 he deployed Shakespeare against the country's current enemy by likening Napoleon Bonaparte to

Macbeth. Coleridge hoped the emperor would end as the regicide did, and warned that England had produced Nelson and Wellington as well as Shakespeare. At the border, the national poet functioned as a territorial sentinel: Shakespeare Cliff near Dover was a frequent subject for Turner's watercolours, in which it mostly consists of white space, as inconceivable as God or its namesake. Never mind that in *King Lear* the cliff is a verbal mirage; for Turner it functioned as a national rampart, confirming the proud insularity described by Imogen in *Cymbeline* when she says that

> I' the world's volume
> Our Britain seems as of it, but not in 't;
> In a great pool a swan's nest.

(Of course, having read Jonson's tribute to Shakespeare, we know the identity of the allegorical swan.)

Inconveniently enough, Cymbeline loosens his grip on what Garrick in his *Ode* called 'Britannia's riches and her force': the vassal king agrees to pay tribute to Rome, even after winning the war against its legions. As Michael Dobson points out, mid-eighteenth-century adaptations by William Hawkins and Garrick altered this meek, compliant outcome and made Cymbeline reject the imperious demand. When Britain acquired an empire of its own, it was Shakespeare who justified the submission of the country's colonies. He ruled, Carlyle said, over 'all Nations of Englishmen', whatever their citizenship, and the name of his birthplace was occasionally doled out as a baptismal gift in the whiter territories. Ontario has a Stratford and an Avon, though they are in Perth County; there is another Stratford on another Avon in the hinterland beyond Melbourne. When the Australian states federated in 1901, a site was chosen for a national capital on grazing land midway between Melbourne and Sydney. One name proposed for this notional city – along with Paradise, Olympus,

Kangaremu and Eucalypta – was Shakespeare; luckily the politicians opted to call it Canberra, which saved it from having to be worthy of God, the gods, or a literary godfather.

In 1918, in an unwitting repetition of Coleridge's threat to Napoleon, T. S. Eliot observed that the British public depended on a ghostly alliance of 'Shakespeare, Nelson, Wellington' – to whose names he added that of Newton – for confirmation of the country's supremacy. Eliot's sly mockery had little effect. An imperial pageant staged at Wembley in 1924 included Elgar's musical setting of 'Shakespeare's Kingdom', a poem by Alfred Noyes which imagines the young man from the Midlands arriving in London during 'England's conquering hour', his knapsack stuffed with 'quiet songs' that surpassed in value the gold in all 'the galleons of th' Armada'. The empire, according to the poem, existed to disseminate Shakespeare, who would outlive it.

Halfway through the nineteenth century, Carlyle wagered that if the English had to choose between granting independence to India or doing without Shakespeare, they would give up the colony. A century later it was the Indians who decided to let Shakespeare go. The Merchant-Ivory film *Shakespeare Wallah*, about a troupe of British actors trekking the plays around the subcontinent in the 1950s, wistfully records this loss of authority. A Maharajah who opens his palace for a very heavily cut performance of *Antony and Cleopatra* interprets Richard II's deposition as an elegy for his rule and for the British Raj. A young Indian playboy whose mistress is a Bollywood dancer goes reluctantly to *Hamlet*, enjoys the fencing match, but is irritated by the hero's procrastination: the ineffectual prince belongs to an outmoded, fuddy-duddy world. Shakespeare's tragedies have recently been invited back, but on India's terms: in Vishai Bhardwaj's films *Maqbool*, *Omkara* and *Haider*, Macbeth becomes a Mumbai gangster, Othello is an underworld enforcer in Uttar Pradesh, and Hamlet battles terrorists in Kashmir.

In the Caribbean, Aimé Césaire from Martinique reworked *The Tempest* in his play *Une Tempête*, staged in Paris in 1969. Shakespeare's Caliban foolishly exchanges one master for another, and ends abjectly suing for grace; Césaire radicalized him, presenting him as a freedom fighter with a justified grievance rather than a lecherous malcontent. He refuses to answer to the name Prospero assigns him, arguing that his identity has been stolen along with his native land: he demands to be called X, like the assassinated Muslim minister Malcolm X, who denounced the United States for its crimes against what Césaire called 'négritude'. Proudly black, Caliban now jeers at the mulatto slave Ariel as an Uncle Tom, and rejects Prospero's talk about civilizing the wilderness, the perennial alibi of profiteers with an eye on raw materials and cheap labour. Yet when he has the chance to kill his despotic boss, he refuses to strike the decisive blow. He is, he says, a rebel but not a murderer – and for a moment he seems even more principled than Shakespeare's Brutus, determined to keep vengeance and violence out of a political dispute.

In South Africa, Shakespeare was read, discussed, and adopted as a guide to resistance by the prisoners of conscience on Robben Island. A volume of the collected plays circulated between cells: its owner Sonny Venkatrathnam pasted greeting cards on its cover as camouflage, fixing them with porridge instead of glue, and told the Afrikaans-speaking warders that it was his Bible, which kept them from interfering. Prisoners in solitary confinement marked favourite passages, then passed the book on as a way of transmitting messages to each other. Billy Nair naturally enough underlined Caliban's 'This island's mine', while Walter Sisulu highlighted Shylock's retort 'For suff'rance is the badge of all our tribe'. Nelson Mandela's selection – made in 1977, a little more than halfway through the twenty-seven years he spent in prison – was the speech in which Caesar ignores advice to stay at home on the ides of March:

Antony and Cleopatra performed at the Maharaja's palace
by the Buckingham Players in *Shakespeare Wallah*.

> Cowards die many times before their deaths;
> The valiant never taste of death but once.

The remark, like most of what Caesar says, is supercilious, scoffing at the self-preservation of lesser men. Taken up by Mandela, who at this stage probably expected to die behind bars, it became a statement of magnificent moral courage, all the more impressive because it was not spoken aloud but intoned silently, thanks to his signature in the margin of the text. Shakespeare may not have guaranteed the adhesion of Britain's colonies but – as ever a maverick – he intellectually armed the rebels who defied and shamed European empires.

*

Shakespeare was always more than a national patrimony. The globe, as Prospero says, belongs impartially to 'all which it inherit', and Britain forfeited its exclusive rights as soon as the plays spread around the world.

In Germany in the late eighteenth century, Shakespeare was recruited for a culture war that pitted the Grecian south against the more vital, expansive Gothic north. Schlegel likened the art of Sophocles to the ideally proportional Parthenon, but said that Shakespeare, with his heaven-storming rhetoric and organically fluent tragicomic form, resembled St Stephen's Cathedral, which grows so steeply and impatiently upwards to tower over Vienna. The English made ineffectual efforts to hold onto him: George Eliot argued that the Germans were incapable of appreciating Shakespeare, and chuckled at their admiration for his Teutonically clumsy wordplay. Stendhal challenged French prejudices in his polemical pamphlet *Racine et Shakespeare*, which ridiculed his compatriots for hissing performances of 'notre pauvre Shakspeare' simply because he came from perfidious Albion. An academician extols Racine as a decorous remnant of the courtly past; a romantic, his opponent in Stendhal's debate, praises Shakespeare as a liberator, in politics as well as art. Italians had no need to overcome national misgivings since Shakespeare, having set plays in Rome, Venice, Verona, Mantua and Sicily, almost enjoyed honorary citizenship. Arrigo Boito, the librettist for Verdi's *Falstaff*, claimed that the opera's Latin gaiety restored the beery sybaritic protagonist to his 'clear Tuscan source' in Boccaccio's *Decameron*, and Borges once proposed half-seriously that Shakespeare might have been Italian – or, failing that, Jewish – because his exuberance seemed so uncharacteristic of the dour English.

In due course the plays were expatriated to 'all Scenes of Europe' and points beyond, reconceived to suit local conditions wherever they touched down. *King Lear* has travelled furthest, perhaps because its calamities are provoked by what Goneril calls 'domestic-door particulars', squabbles that are current in every human community – generational friction, sibling rivalry, the apportionment of family spoils, even tantrums about housekeeping. Kingship is incidental to the play, or can be a byword for fatherhood; the landscapes that Lear describes when carving up his realm are like unvisited real estate in a brochure – Goneril gets 'plenteous rivers and wide-skirted meads', Regan receives a swathe of territory 'no less in space, validity, and pleasure' – so they are easily replaced by different vistas, or by city streets.

Dethroned and uprooted, Lear reappeared first in Balzac's Paris in *Père Goriot*, then on the plains of Eurasian Russia in Turgenev's *A Lear of the Steppes*, a story about a landowner of Herculean bulk who is mistreated by his two grasping daughters. In the play, Lear threatens to do things that will be 'the terrors of the earth', though he has no idea what those enormities might be. Turgenev's Harlov makes good on the boast when he demolishes a house with his bare hands, prising nails out of the roof and tossing beams aside. Lear breaks up his kingdom without a second thought, and is not bothered by the warfare that ensues. Harlov, more truly monarchical in his thinking than Lear, raves about exterminating evil Tartars and thieving Lithuanians. After his death, one daughter administers his estate with stringent discipline, the other joins a flagellating religious cult: between them they hint at two equally baleful Russian futures, totalitarian or mystical. At least Goneril and Regan have the decency to die while squabbling over Edmund.

Turgenev's narrator introduces his homegrown Lear while discussing Shakespeare's 'types' with some friends, who comment on the Hamlets, Falstaffs, Othellos, Richard IIIs and Macbeths of their acquaintance. The trouble with such categories is that nobody in Shakespeare is typical: Philostrate points out that the mechanicals in *A Midsummer Night's Dream* have chosen to labour in their minds not with their hands, and the cobbler and carpenter in *Julius Caesar* annoy the tribunes because they refuse to display the menial emblems of their trades. Although the characters Turgenev mentions came to be seen as representatives of eternal human traits, they began as unique, paradoxical creations – an intellectual aristocrat, a melancholy fat man, a psychologically fragile warrior, a witty killer, a murderer whose crimes are promoted by metaphysical or even spiritual curiosity. It was Johnson who first saw Shakespeare's people as prototypes, 'the genuine progeny of common humanity, such as the world will always supply, and observation will always find'. Once that typology was established, writers eagerly identified or invented new examples, and these 'allegorical beings' – as Boswell called the participants in the Jubilee pageant – spawned offshoots that in time strayed far from Europe.

Akira Kurosawa's film *Ran* identifies a Japanese analogue for Lear in Shakespeare's own period, during a time of strife between feudal chieftains who as yet were restrained by no central power. The retirement of the warlord Hidetora provokes his three male heirs into fratricidal combat, and as their colour-coded bands of samurai charge into battle, the story swells into a meditation on history and its helpless repetitions. Corpses pile up, as in Tokyo after the 1923 earthquake or in bombed Hiroshima in 1945. Kurosawa's sixteenth-century characters are forever glancing apprehensively at a sky in which clouds resemble nuclear puffballs, straining to explode. Blood spurts in pressurized jets, or drips through the floorboards of a besieged castle like rain from a leaky roof; severed heads, packed in salt because of the summer heat, are traded as trophies of war. But this carnage is contemplated from afar, without provoking the churned-up, overwrought response elicited by the horrors in *King Lear*: Kurosawa's soundtrack muffles the shouts, shots and metallic clatter of battle, and the numbing effect implies that the conflict is ineradicable and interminable. One victim bears no grudge towards Hidetora, even though he has slaughtered her family and burned their castle. As a Buddhist, she believes that everything is determined by past lives that we are currently re-enacting. Perhaps the karma to which she refers is a synonym for the predestining influence of Shakespeare.

Lear visits the Kenyan highlands in Karen Blixen's memoir *Out of Africa*, although he does so only as Blixen prepares to leave her farm and return to Denmark. When she worries about the future of some squatters on her land, a British colonial functionary in Nairobi tells her there is 'no real need' for them to stay. Blixen's unspoken rejoinder is 'O, reason not the need!', which is Lear's response when Regan questions the number of his retainers. She imagines the natives struggling to understand a new dispensation that will leave them wondering where they are, and this prompts another reminiscence of the play: when Lear asks if he is in France, Kent replies 'In your own kingdom, sir'. *King Lear* here tells the story of those supplanted Kenyan tribes, with Shakespeare's latter-day compatriots as the villains. So much for the imperial mission propounded in Garrick's *Ode*, which promised to make the 'precious freight' of the plays available to 'the envious nations'.

Lear's longest journey has taken him to Australia. In Patrick White's novel *The Eye of the Storm* he becomes the domineering matriarch Elizabeth Hunter, whose storm is a tropical cyclone on an island off the Queensland coast. Unlike Lear, she is responsible for the weather: she represents the maenadic madness of a force we temperately personify as Mother Nature. As she lies dying, her son Basil – a knighted actor who, like many of his colleagues, has fallen short when attempting to play Lear in London – interrupts his vigil at her bedside by taking a side trip to the bush, where he tests Shakespeare against the lacerating glare of 'the Australian daylight'. In the novel, he recites Lorenzo's moonlit speech from *The Merchant of Venice*; when Fred Schepisi filmed the book, he substituted one of Lear's irate outbursts on the heath. Geoffrey Rush, cast as Basil, starts the speech while paddling into a mucky dam where he once fished during childhood holidays, but the excerpt breaks off with a non-Shakespearean cry of 'Oh shit shit shit' as he treads on broken glass or rusty tin and gashes his foot. A wide-angled view reduces Basil to a puny insect in the hot dry waste, with magpies chorally disparaging the poetry that he booms into the void. White brought Shakespeare to Australia, but could not make him stay.

King Lear has planted a more permanent stake in American soil, initially in two Westerns directed by Anthony Mann that resituate the play in New Mexico. Mann's Lear in *The Furies* is a cattle baron, so regal that he even prints his own currency for use on his immense ranch. His adoring but incestuously jealous daughter – a compound of Cordelia and her vicious sisters, played by Barbara Stanwyck – attacks a would-be stepmother with a pair of scissors. Reviled by her father as 'a canker to be cut out', she schemes to ruin him by buying up his worthless IOUs. No armies are involved: the war is financial. *The Man from Laramie* concerns an elderly rancher with failing sight who has a quarrelsome pair of male heirs, which makes him as much Gloucester as Lear. But the torture that is the film's equivalent to the blinding of Gloucester happens to a former army officer, played by James Stewart, who is investigating the illicit sale of rifles to the Apaches. The rancher's sadistic son pinions him with arms outstretched, then shoots him in the hand he uses for firing his gun. In the trigger-happy West, that is as disabling as the loss of his eyes would be.

The Lear in Tennessee Williams's *Cat on a Hot Tin Roof* is the Mississippi Delta patriarch Big Daddy Pollitt – another small-scale monarch whose realm is 28,000 acres of swamp that he has transformed into pasture. Big Daddy, unlike Lear, has no intention of giving up his domain; instead he plans to build a textile mill so he can weave the cotton he grows and then market it. Whereas Lear acts with terrifying unexpectedness, Williams explains Big Daddy as the logical product of a society dedicated to conspicuous consumption: he is said to be greedily over-compensating for an impoverished childhood, buying up land while gorging on candied yams. We know nothing about Lear's queen, the mother of those vexatious daughters. Williams, however, fills in the details of Big Daddy's marital history and his extra-marital itches. His loud, fat consort Big Mama has provided him with the two sons he needed to establish a dynasty: daughters would have been unacceptable, because he could not entrust the business to them. Now he fantasizes about taking a mistress, whom he intends to smother with minks and choke with diamonds. He assesses his daughters-in-law as 'breeders', but comes nowhere near Lear's obscene curse on Goneril's 'organs of increase'.

When Lear suggests anatomizing Regan, he means it metaphorically. Big Daddy, however, has been clinically anatomized, and a surgeon reveals that his spastic colon is actually a cancer that has 'gone past the knife'. Disease takes the place of the moral flaws that bring down the heroes of classical tragedy, which leaves open the possibility of recovery or at least palliation. Like Nahum Tate, Williams recoils from the random, unmitigated anguish with which *King Lear* concludes, and Big Daddy's physician leaves him a merciful supply of morphine. One day, perhaps, American medical research may find a cure for tragedy.

*

Uninhibited by the deference that prevails elsewhere, Americans have often wondered why Shakespeare had the misfortune to be born on another continent.

An ode by Peter Markoe, published in 1787 in Philadelphia, serves as a declaration of independence for Shakespeare, who is prised out of the 'narrow bounds' of 'monopolizing Britain' and naturalized on 'our western shore', which is the world's 'noblest Stage'. After the migratory voyage of Shakespeare's 'bold spirit', his goods and chattels might have followed: in 1844 the circus impresario P. T. Barnum considered buying up his Stratford birthplace so he could display it – along with a mermaid, a bearded lady, a pair of Siamese twins, and the trunk of a tree under which Christ's disciples had once sat – in the museum he had opened in New York. The house remained in England, but Washington DC now has the world's largest Shakespeare collection, assembled by Henry Clay Folger, who bequeathed his library to the nation in 1932. Folger's widow said that he regarded Shakespeare as 'one of the wells from which we Americans draw our national thought, our faith and our hope'. The image of the well is apt: Folger was an oil executive. Shakespeare's language has much in common with the gushers of black gold that enriched the stockholders of Standard Oil, which was Folger's company; whether the plays underpin a national ideology is another matter.

Walt Whitman thought that America was better off without Shakespeare, because the greasy rabble in *Coriolanus* and the illiterate thugs who follow Cade in *Henry VI* insulted 'the pride and dignity of the common people'. Rioters protesting against this feudal snobbery called a halt to William Charles Macready's performance of *Macbeth* in New York in 1849; the militia had to be summoned, and there were multiple deaths. Yet in 1850 Emerson predicted that Shakespeare would continue to nourish 'the foremost people of the world', by which he meant 'the Saxon race' on both sides of the Atlantic. Americans of non-Saxon derivation also expected a share: in 1903 in *The Souls of Black Folk* W. E. B. Du Bois said 'I sit with Shakespeare and he winces not.'

Du Bois, who was campaigning for racial equality in college education, here made Shakespeare synonymous with the high culture to which he rightfully demanded access; in America, however, it was Shakespeare's happy fate to be absorbed into a lower, less exclusive culture. *Kiss Me, Kate*, the musical Cole Porter based on *The Taming of the Shrew*, includes a duet for two literate heavies who brush up their Shakespeare while waiting to maul a victim in the alley outside a Broadway theatre. Porter's elastic rhymes put the titles of the plays to new and impudent uses. The gangsters mock clipped, pukka speech by quoting *Troilus and Cressida* to 'the wife of the British embessida'. When an offended woman calls them 'heinous' they 'kick her right in the *Coriolanus*', and a floozy's 'plea for pleasure' earns her the chance to 'sample [their] *Measure for Measure*'. The slangy lewdness is authentically Shakespearean: words, as Feste points out, are shamelessly corruptible.

A short film called *Shake, Mr Shakespeare*, made in 1936, shows the stiff, elderly literary characters emerging from their incarceration in leathery books to engage in the pursuit of American happiness. Hamlet sets up Yorick's long bones as pins in a bowling alley and uses his skull as a ball to knock them down,

overleaf
The army of Hidetora's son Jiro, Great Lord of
the Ichimongi clan, in Kurosawa's *Ran*.

an Othello in blackface forgets his marital woes and tries out one of Al Jolson's minstrel routines, and Cleopatra's serpentine acrobatics with two muscle men hint at her coital accomplishments. The moony Juliet ignores the advice of her Nurse to 'read a good book' and instead sings a disconsolate torch song; rebuffed, Romeo vows to 'knock that dame right off her balcony'. Shakespeare himself tries to re-impose good manners, but a jelly-bellied Falstaff coaxes him to shake it up by jitterbugging. Another set of democratized Shakespearean characters is evoked in Duke Ellington's *Such Sweet Thunder*, composed after his trip to the Shakespeare festival in Stratford, Ontario in 1956. A ragtime waltz for Lady Macbeth harks back to what Ellington assumes was her seductive youth. In 'Up and Down, Up and Down' Puck's trumpet jeers at the orchestrated mayhem of the other instruments in Ellington's band, and in 'Madness in Great Ones' the same free-associating trumpet traces the insane mental arabesques of Hamlet: jazz with its riffs matches the high-flying virtuosity of Shakespeare's language.

'Shakespeare was not meant for taverns', sniffs the affronted thespian Granville Thorndyke in John Ford's Western *My Darling Clementine*, indignant because he has been obliged to recite 'To be, or not to be' in a saloon. His disdain is misplaced: Hamlet welcomes Rosencrantz and Guildenstern to Elsinore by promising to teach them to 'drink deep ere you depart'. The saloon's patrons fire their guns at Thorndyke's feet to make him dance; when he retreats, the consumptive Doc Holliday continues the soliloquy, until his performance too is curtailed by a coughing fit. Ford's film first puts Hamlet's speech to the test by having the actor recite its philosophical ramblings as he farcically dodges bullets, then allows it to fall apart as the words are broken up by Holliday's spluttering, a symptom of his fatal illness. Both the harried actor and the ailing doctor are closer to death than Hamlet is when he debates the rights and wrongs of self-slaughter. How could this play not belong in a town called Tombstone, built in the geological cemetery of Monument Valley?

Out West, Shakespeare's dramatic conflicts ricochet through ample, unsettled space, and characters can escape from tragedy by travelling on to a new life beyond the horizon. *Jubal*, a Western directed by Delmer Daves, avoids a Shakespearean dead end by looking at *Othello* from the guiltless Cassio's point of view. The foreman Jubal is maligned by an Iago-like ranch hand, and also compromised by the boss's wife, a predatory Desdemona (who comes from Canada, which presumably is meant to explain her low morals). He kills his employer in self-defence when unjustly accused – what might have happened if Cassio had stood up to Othello? – but has committed no crime because a judge rules that it was a fair fight. Released from custody, he rides off with a family of Mormon pilgrims who just happen to be passing. On the plains of Wyoming, the snowy Grand Tetons are the gateway to a promised land.

Back East, an American city proved to be as wide open as the frontier or the woodland to which comic characters resort in *The Merry Wives of Windsor*, *A Midsummer Night's Dream* or *As You Like It*. During the 1950s, when Jack Kerouac and Allen Ginsberg came to the intersection of Broadway and 42nd Street in New York, they sometimes saluted Times Square by announcing 'This is the forest of Arden'. With an upbeat American inflection, the comment cast off the doleful tone it possesses for the exiled Rosalind. Kerouac saw the neon-afforested crossroads as 'the crux of life', with 'dense masses of people going about all their ways of being'; adding a Shakespearean pun, he described his ideal society as a 'Garden of Arden, full of lovers and louts'. America can accommodate all those questers, whatever their provenance, and is able to distribute them throughout its diversified landscapes. 'Somewhere', as the lovers in *West Side Story* sing, 'there's a place for us', a haven that will offer this Romeo and Juliet of the New York slums a 'peace and quiet and open air' that are unavailable in Shakespeare's fractious Verona and give them the chance to enjoy 'a new way of living' – the recurring motif of American Utopianism.

Shakespeare supplies no cause for the enmity of the families in *Romeo and Juliet*: as the drama's donnée, it can be left unexplained, like Iago's motiveless malice. The gang warfare in *West Side Story* is a social problem, soluble by the demolition of tenements and a Civics lesson in tolerance and togetherness. Leonard Bernstein and Stephen Sondheim found urban equivalents for Shakespeare's settings – a dance in a school gym replaces a courtly ball, a fire escape stands in for Juliet's balcony, and the apothecary's shop is a musty, under-stocked drugstore, where the avuncular proprietor Doc dispenses soda and candy and certainly has no supply of poison under the counter. In its absence, there can be no double suicide; Tony is shot but Maria survives to deliver a healing homily that condemns bigotry and violence.

Tragedy, with its claustrophobic enclosure and its limited choices, remains unwelcome in the land of the free. Although Peter Markoe's ode invoked Shakespeare's 'soul-harrowing name' and relished the 'pleasing horror' it induced, he treated the plays as parables of justice and righteousness, as in a couplet that over-tidily summarizes *Richard III* and *Hamlet*:

> A nation's woe the warlike Richmond fires;
> A father's death the gallant prince inspires.

Later American adaptations and commentaries bring the same meliorism to bear. Either the tragic character is reprieved, as in *Jubal*, or else his transgressive hubris is downgraded by something like a plea deal. In an essay written in 1962, Mary McCarthy described Macbeth as a murderous version of Babbitt, the suburban bore from Middle America in Sinclair Lewis's satirical novel; his blandness, she argued, is evident from his first remark in the play, which is chitchat about the weather. 'He is literal-minded,' McCarthy says when pointing out how stupid he is to trust the fortune-telling witches; 'that, in a word, is his tragedy.' Surely his tragedy has more to do with his nightmarish imagination and the exquisitely painful sensitivity that makes his infractions, in his own eyes, so unforgivable? But McCarthy's essay was an oblique attempt to explain the bureaucratic conformism of the Pentagon generals who fought America's imperial wars in Asia, and the blundering of these uniformed dunces left her unable to recognize any evil that was not banal.

With the same populist aim, Ben Affleck recently called Batman 'the American version of Hamlet'. True, young Bruce Wayne was traumatized by the murder of his parents, and he adopts a caped and cowled bat suit – an inky cloak by other means – as his disguise while he fights crime in Gotham City. But the Hamlet who affects madness and creates chaos is closer to Batman's eternal opponent, the Joker. America's compulsory optimism intervenes again in Affleck's remark, this time turning Shakespeare's morally queasy, spiritually perplexed protagonist into an impeccable superhero.

*

It is the cinema that has made Shakespeare a citizen of the world, effectively globalizing him.

Silent films bypassed nationality by excluding language. They relied on the emoting of the body or the semaphore of facial expressions, at which Shakespeare's characters were as adept as Chaplin or Garbo: Prospero's spirits gesticulate in an 'excellent dumb discourse' when laying the banquet table, and Romeo, interpreting Juliet's glances, says 'She speaks, yet she says nothing'. Mimed excerpts from the plays were filmed as early as 1899, three decades before synchronized sound. The King John of Herbert Beerbohm Tree twitchily dies in his chair in one of the first fragments; in an American abbreviation of *A Midsummer Night's Dream* made in 1909, a female Puck performs harmless tricks during a mild-mannered daylight picnic, with no hint of erotic hysteria.

Cut loose from the authorized text, the voiceless characters of silent film sneakily augmented or altered Shakespeare's plots. In an *Othello* from Germany in 1922, a title card reports that the Moor has told the Venetian senators that he is the son of an Egyptian prince and a Spanish princess. He needs that pedigree, having been deprived of Shakespeare's ennobling poetry: without its support, Emil Jannings looks buffoonish. He indulges in some heavy-handed horseplay with Desdemona in her bedroom, and when Emilia interrupts he twists her inside a curtain to stop her from spying on their connubial romp. Action over-compensates for the lack of words. In the play, Iago says that he intends to 'make my fool my purse'; Werner Krauss's Iago acts out the metaphor, nimbly pocketing Roderigo's remaining funds with one hand while he eats his lunch with the other. He messily hurls the plate of food away when accused of double-dealing, then adjusts the curly ends of his moustache to denote malevolence. Cassio's dream about sex with Desdemona, which in the play is Iago's invention, is here given to Othello. While he writhes on his bed in a torment of jealousy, the literally filmy figures of his wife and her suspected lover flicker above him, embracing. Though his eyes are closed, does this count as the 'ocular proof' he demands?

The cinema's aim is to make fantasies materialize, as it does in this scene from *Othello*, and when Max Reinhardt filmed his lushly arboreal production of *A Midsummer Night's Dream* in 1935, Shakespeare's enchanted wood merged with Hollywood's industrial phantasmagoria. Inside a hangar at the studio – Mab's cave with the benefit of the latest technology – the forest was stocked with an avenue of athletic human trees and an orchestra of bug-eyed gnomes. A mud-encrusted toad with an old man's face surfaces from a pond, fireflies swarm in the gloaming, and Oberon is surrounded by an entourage of agitated leathery bats. A grizzly bear and a hog have walk-ons, and a unicorn serves as the Indian prince's pet pony. Reinhardt added to the play a wordless nocturne in which demons round up the gossamer-winged fairies, usher them under Oberon's billowing black cape and hustle them away before dawn. Choreographed by Bronislawa Nijinksa, with Mendelssohn's incidental music sombrely re-orchestrated by Erich Wolfgang Korngold, the sequence illustrates the cinema's Manichean combat between night and day, as the darkness in which we do our dreaming is pierced by a light beam from the projector that slices through the gloom and animates phantoms. When Puck in his farewell refers to the fairies as 'we shadows', he defines the bodies that have an ectoplasmic or undead life on celluloid; the rest of us – to adapt his words – half-slumber as images shimmer on a screen inside our heads.

In *Everybody's Shakespeare*, an edition of the plays that he recorded for radio during the 1930s, Orson Welles encouraged amateur performances 'in a class-room, a gymnasium, a dance-hall or a back-yard'. On film, Welles took Shakespeare further afield. After a *Macbeth* that recycled the set previously used for a coalmine in several low-rent Westerns, Welles went on location to Venice and Morocco for *Othello*, and made *Chimes at Midnight*, his version of *Henry IV*, in crumbling castles throughout Spain. When Olivier filmed his Old Vic production of *Henry V*, he chose to begin inside the Globe at a gaffe-prone, rain-soaked matinee. Then, during one of the speeches by the Chorus – acts of evocation that the critic James Agee called 'verbal movies' – the performance takes flight cinematically, and we watch from high above as the army of invasion crosses to France; the film expands into the open air for the battle, shot in 1943 in Ireland with local soldiers as

overleaf
Victor Jory as Oberon and Sheila Brown as the Indian prince
in Max Reinhardt's film of *A Midsummer Night's Dream*.

extras. At the end we are returned to the theatre with an alienating jolt, and curtain calls expose the French princess as a gawky adolescent boy in a curly wig.

Subsequent directors have seldom attempted to squeeze the genie back into the bottle: now what matters is to find camera-ready locations that suit the plays. All the world's a backlot, and all the men and women merely extras.

Hamlet, confined to the studio in Olivier's version, has since been filmed by Peter Brook in bleak North Jutland and by Grigori Kozintsev in a grim, paranoid fortress on the Estonian coast, then more picturesquely by Franco Zeffirelli at Dover Castle and by Kenneth Branagh in and around the baroque pile of Blenheim Palace. Michael Almereyda set his *Hamlet* on the upper floors and terraces of a Manhattan skyscraper, with an expedition to street level for Ethan Hawke, who mutters 'To be, or not be' while browsing through the shelves of movies labelled ACTION at Blockbuster Video but, inevitably indecisive, does not make a purchase. For his *Richard III* Richard Loncraine chose London monuments that look sombrely Gothic or oppressively fascist: St Pancras railway hotel or Battersea power station. Trevor Nunn filmed *Twelfth Night* on the rocky promontories of Victorian Cornwall: where better to wreck a ship? Branagh took *Much Ado About Nothing* on holiday to a Tuscan villa, which allowed for picnics, strolls beneath the pergola, conspiratorial plotting in the wine cellar, and a naked romp in a water tank for the strapping young soldiers; capitalizing on the popularity of the region, Michael Hoffmann moved *A Midsummer Night's Dream* from Athens to the hill town of Montepulciano, which for the sake of appearances he renamed Monte Athena. Shortly before the war in Kosovo, Julie Taymor used a Roman amphitheatre in Croatia for the victory rally in her version of *Titus Andronicus*, and Ralph Fiennes later filmed *Coriolanus* in Belgrade, after auditioning Bucharest, Zagreb and Sarajevo – all places scarred by recent conflict, which authenticated these dramas of imperial disintegration.

Metaphors are transporters, and a fancied affinity is enough to justify dispatching Shakespeare to long-haul destinations. Taymor filmed her *Tempest* on a volcanic island in Hawaii that looks freshly created by the alchemy of fire, as if one of Prospero's spells had commanded those spars of charred black rock to protrude from the Pacific, and smoggy Mexico City proves a suitably febrile habitat for the thumb-biting, hot-rodding, pill-popping, gun-toting teenagers in Baz Luhrmann's *Romeo + Juliet*. Everybody's Shakespeare thrives everywhere.

And This Gives Life to Thee

Classics and antiques
Acting royally
Anachronisms
The past is prologue
Merely players

In the epitaph above his grave in the Stratford church, Shake-speare asks that his dust should not be dug and puts a curse on 'he that moves my bones'. Whether or not he desired unmolested oblivion, he expected his sonnets to outlast marble, gilded mon-uments, and 'unswept stone besmeared with sluttish time'. The eighteenth in the sequence advertises its endurance – 'So long lives this' – after which, more altruistically, it adds 'and this gives life to thee'. The sonnets often conclude with such complimentary truisms; this one happens to be true.

That life-giving pledge to the poem's addressee extends to each of us when we read it, and it goes further if we recite it to someone else. While writing this book I attended a lunch to celebrate the thirtieth wedding anniversary of two friends. Since they are both Shakespeareans, it took place in Stratford, with a plump pink Falstaffian bust of the man himself keeping watch from a window ledge. At the end of his speech, the husband paid tribute to his wife by quoting Shakespeare's 116th sonnet, the one that provided Samuel Colman with the title for his painting of Doomsday. The poem's subject is not Armageddon but 'the marriage of true minds', and the motto extracted from it on this occasion was 'Love's not Time's fool'. It is a bold claim, especially if you remember that Hotspur's dying words define life as time's fool: all Shakespearean statements are subjective and relative, the opinion of whoever voices them rather than universal rules. Nevertheless, raising a glass, our host asked all those present to repeat the motto. In unison we did so, which made the assertion personal; that chorus, followed by laughter and applause, voted down poor Hotspur's pessimism.

Unlike his sonnets, Shakespeare's plays were hostages to time, and he may have assumed that they would be forgotten when his company of actors stopped performing them, like early films left to decay in their canisters or burn up when the cellulose caught fire. Instead they have been given protected status as cultural treasures, and prescribed almost medicinally for generations of students – yet despite the burden of prestige and the educational grind, they have never lost their power to amaze, surprise and even shock. Prompting us to both think and feel, often simultaneously, they give life to us; we return the gift when we speculate about the conduct of Shakespeare's characters or respond to their rhetorical questions. 'Whoever loved that loved not at first sight?' asks Phebe in *As You Like It*. 'Can I do this,' demands the future Richard III after boasting of his devilish political skills, 'and cannot get a crown?' She knows that we will nod in wistful or contented agreement; he suspects that we will secretly encourage him to eliminate more of his obstructive relatives. Antagonism can be just as enlivening as assent: the director Katie Mitchell has condemned Hamlet as an abuser and declared that our sympathy should go to Ophelia. You may disagree, but the argument is about living beings, who solicit our support or need our protection.

Treating Shakespeare as a classic relegates him to something like the non-existent 'golden world' where the exiled courtiers in Arden are said, quite wrongly, to be fleetly amusing themselves. An exhibition in Stratford to mark his quatercentenary in 1964 installed him in just such an aureate heyday. The catalogue opened with an essay on the wealth, grandeur and global swagger of the Elizabethan era, which it called a long-ago 'golden morning', when England had 'a two hundred years' start over the rest of Europe'. At the exhibition's entrance, a suspended clock with arrows pointing in all directions spirited visitors out of the depleted present: 'The Traveller', the guidebook awkwardly explained, 'arrives through Time back to the year of Shakespeare's birth.'

Such chronic nostalgia was unknown in 1564. For Shakespeare the word 'antique' is temptingly close to its homonym 'antic', meaning chaotic or grotesque, as in Hamlet's 'antic disposition' or

overleaf
Ethan Hawke at Blockbuster Video
in Michael Almereyda's film of *Hamlet*.

'the wild disguise' that Octavius in *Antony and Cleopatra* says has 'almost / Antickt us all'. In the sixteenth century, something ancient was not necessarily dignified and venerable; it might simply be absurd or incomprehensible because obsolete. It could even be fusty, morbid, fatal, which is why Richard II in his meditation on the mortality of kings calls death 'the antic'.

But whenever English society is unsettled by change, traditions are invented to steady it, and at such times the arts are expected to produce facsimiles of a supposedly stable past. This happened after 1660 during the recovery from political unrest, when Shakespeare was rewritten into classical respectability; it happened again during the social turbulence of the industrial revolution, when the plays were turned into hallowed heirlooms, aged by an extra coat of varnish. A pictorial edition of *Macbeth* by the designer John Moyr Smith, published in 1899, is a late example. It makes a museum piece of the play: the witches confer among Druidical remains that are modelled on a ring of stones in Orkney, and mix their potions in a Danish pot dating from 'the later Bronze age'. Smith provides embroidered table-covers for the banquet that the delirious Macbeth disrupts, and saves the guests from barbarism by issuing them, as he pointed out in a footnote, with 'forks as well as knives'.

At the start of the nineteenth century, as this antiquarian asphyxiation of Shakespeare began, the architectural draughtsman William Capon painted a series of medieval and Tudor backdrops for use in the history plays, with crenellated turrets, Gothic chapels, a market cross at the centre of what Capon called 'a Great Ancient Street', and a restored Tower of London in which the princes in *Richard III* could be murdered. In 1823 Charles Kemble's production of *King John* issued theatregoers with a list of the sources for the thirteenth-century sheaths of mail, armorial shields and cylindrical helmets worn by the barons. Queen Victoria closely monitored such details: so long as the characters were properly attired, she could overlook their king-killing and their other aberrant conduct. After seeing *Macbeth* at Windsor Castle in 1853, she recalled in her diary 'the dresses beautiful, & most correct', and following a performance of *The Winter's Tale* in 1856 she reported that Prince Albert was 'in ecstasies' over 'the splendid & strictly correct antique costumes, all taken from the best works & models'. Costumery became a selling point for Henry Irving's *Henry VIII*, which in 1892 promised 'a succession of historical pictures', with 'every ruff, head-dress, sword-belt, shoe' copied from verified originals. Beerbohm Tree staged the same play in 1910 as a pageant that displayed 'the manners and customs of that great age', and cut half the text to leave room for slow-moving parades of Tudor finery.

By then, as Bernard Shaw complained, the stage had become 'an optical illusion' that audiences looked at 'through a huge hole in the wall' – not a mirror but a telescope aimed backwards down the diminishing vista of the centuries. In 1936 George Cukor's film of *Romeo and Juliet* was described as a 'picturization', a term then applied to cinematic adaptations of the most esteemed and elderly literary properties. The credit titles unfurl on parchment, and the prologue begins as an illustrated page with the texture of needlepoint: the figure of a courtier gradually stirs into life, delivers his choral introduction from a scroll, then reverts to his stitched pose. The competing militias of the Montagues and Capulets, uniformed in brocaded liveries copied from the Magi in a Florentine fresco by Benozzo Gozzoli, trade insults in a square that manages to cram in most of Verona's churches, along with a bustling market that was thought to be picturesque. Despite this urban setting, the middle-aged lovers are put out to pasture. Leslie Howard's Romeo moons in a meadow with a flock of sheep, and Norma Shearer's Juliet cuddles a faun that wears a jewelled collar. Doves preen and coo ubiquitously.

The play, so violent in its physical and verbal delights, is treated here with hushed, almost funereal respect. Fittingly, Romeo and Juliet are to be transformed after death into replicas of themselves in 'pure gold', and when Montague predicts that in Verona 'There shall no figure at such rate be set / As that of true and faithful Juliet', his former enemy Capulet volunteers to pay for a corresponding effigy, so that 'rich shall Romeo's by his lady's lie'. Those sculptures will serve as tokens of lasting fame and undiminished value, which is what Montague means by 'rate': classics are priceless, culture's gold standard. Cukor's film ends with the ceremonious sealing of the tomb, an added bit of business that might possibly recall the anathema in the Stratford church – except that it was Shakespeare who created the clowning gravediggers at Elsinore and wrote the humorous repartee they exchange while they disturb Yorick's dust and unsettle his bones.

*

Classics belong on pedestals, out of reach like the images of Shakespeare by Scheemakers, Roubiliac and Gower. As if such homages were not enough, Shakespeare has suffered another kind of dignified paralysis: he has been enthroned. In his lifetime he enjoyed royal patronage, and following the accession of James I in 1603 his theatre company renamed itself The King's Men. By the mid-eighteenth century he needed no such warrant. Garrick's *Ode* imagined him as an aesthetic despot, 'sitting on his magic throne, / Unaided and alone', with the human passions prostrate at his feet, 'foaming, trembling' in their eagerness to 'own him for their Lord'. A century later, Carlyle celebrated his 'crowned sovereignty' and bowed to him as 'King Shakespeare'.

In the catalogue for the 1964 exhibition in Stratford, the historian Mary St Clare Byrne rousingly coupled Elizabeth I and Shakespeare, whom she acclaimed for 'representing England' as 'partners in greatness'. The partners never actually met, although in *Henry VIII* Cranmer praises the new-born Elizabeth in a speech of astral prophecy that is a sneaky parody of political rhetoric at its most fulsome. The partnership was at last wishfully consummated in Clemence Dane's poetic drama *Will Shakespeare: An Invention*, staged in 1922. Here Elizabeth summons Shakespeare out of premature retirement in Stratford, tells him about her constitutional cares and emotional tribulations, then enlists him for her imperial enterprise. They both launch ships, she says – hers to open trading routes, his bound 'to the hidden lands of the soul' – and he is enjoined to 'Send out your thoughts as I send out my men, / To earn a world for England!' 'Why else', she asks, 'were we two born?'

Judi Dench's Elizabeth I in *Shakespeare in Love* is less world-historically exigent. During a command performance of *Two Gentlemen of Verona*, she enjoys the capers of Crab the dog and tosses him a treat from the meal she is eating, after which she nods off. Elizabeth II did not renew the partnership with Shakespeare. At the opening of the National Theatre's premises on the South Bank in 1976, she attended a performance of Goldoni's *Il Campiello*, a trifling farce about Italian urban life that was mounted for the occasion after Buckingham Palace let it be known that *Hamlet*, then in repertory with Albert Finney, might be too long a sit for the royal party. The queen later allegedly blamed Shakespeare for the haughty affectations of Margaret Thatcher, whose accent she is said to have classified as 'Royal Shakespeare Company received pronunciation from circa 1950'.

Despite such snubs, the alliance between court and stage has lasted through the centuries, with each imitating the other: monarchy is an acting role, and classical actors are inevitably rewarded with redundant aristocratic titles. 'Shakespeare', as the young T. S. Eliot said in a review, 'is the avenue to Knighthood' – a preparation for it as well as a qualification. Aware that performance is impermanent, the theatre has established a hereditary lineage of its own. From Garrick to Kean and on to Henry Irving, Shakespeare's great parts have belonged to a succession of 'king actors', autocrats with stentorian voices – tyrants rather than lovers, to use the distinction Bottom makes when he is offered the role of Pyramus. In Peter Barnes's play *Jubilee*, a satirical survey of commemorations at Stratford since 1769, Garrick becomes a one-man dynasty, anthologizing five Shakespearean reigns in a single speech. He hobbles crookedly as Richard III, dolefully lolls on the ground as Richard II, leaps upright to orate as Henry V, skulks in alarm as King John, and guffaws with hands on hips and legs wide apart as Henry VIII.

The actor-managers who followed Garrick had no scruples about exercising their royal prerogative, even if this meant slighting Shakespeare. Irving insisted on playing Shylock as a blameless man of principle who is double-crossed by hypocritical Christians; after his exit from the court, any return to Belmont would have been anti-climactic, so Irving excised the last act of the play. Beerbohm Tree's productions famously featured interpolations that Shaw called 'swanproof'. As Falstaff, he rode onstage astride a very sturdy white horse; as Richard II, he suppressed a sob when his pet dog sidled over to Bolingbroke and licked the usurper's hand.

Authority for such performers depended on physique: they had to look regal, which is an unfair demand to make of actual monarchs. After seeing John Gielgud as Romeo in 1924, the critic Ivor Brown declared that he possessed 'the most meaningless legs imaginable', which counted as a serious defect. Olivier established his right to the succession by padding his calves before he donned tights. As the introverted Hamlet, he relished a single opportunity for athletic display, and hurled himself into the fencing match with swashbuckling abandon. Inherited accessories maintained the royal line. Gielgud's mother – a niece of Ellen Terry, Irving's leading lady – had given him a sword used by Kean and Irving in

Richard III; in 1944, in an act of noblesse oblige, Gielgud presented the prop to Olivier, who was then performing the role for the first time. But king actors are killers, and when Olivier filmed the play he cast Gielgud as Clarence, who is unceremoniously drowned on Richard's orders after one mournful soliloquy.

Actors still accept knighthoods, but they no longer approach Shakespeare quite so monarchically. Notwithstanding his hump, his limp, his lank hair and his vulpine mouth, Olivier gave Richard III a slinky, twisted seductiveness; when Antony Sher prepared his grotesquely contorted Richard III in 1984, he resolved not to rely on royal charisma, however sinister. Researching Richard's deformity, Sher wondered whether he might attribute the symptoms of coeliac disease to the spidery ogre he was in the process of becoming. 'Play him smelly?' he mused in his diary. Divinity, not body odour, is supposed to hedge a Shakespearean king, but Sher demonstrated that great acting can derive from self-disgust as well from the self-satisfaction that his predecessors exuded.

In 1953 Marlon Brando's sweaty, surly Antony in Joseph Mankiewicz's film of *Julius Caesar* broke with British tradition and introduced a more demotic, cinematically confidential Shakespearean manner – although Gielgud, who played Cassius in the film, winced at Brando's uncontrolled vocal dynamics and wondered whether he might be 'imitating Larry'. During Antony's funeral oration, Brando turns away, pretending to calm his distress while he uses the pause to tease his audience in the forum. The camera – able to see things from all angles and focal lengths, unlike a playgoer in an assigned seat – waits behind him to capture an unseen smirk that telegraphs his cynical enjoyment of his demagoguery. For decades, the theatre resisted this mode of psychological espionage. But when Sam Mendes directed *Richard III* in 2011 at the Old Vic, he used video simulcasts to offer covert glimpses of Richard's reactions, which allowed Kevin Spacey to

overleaf
Glenda Jackson as King Lear.

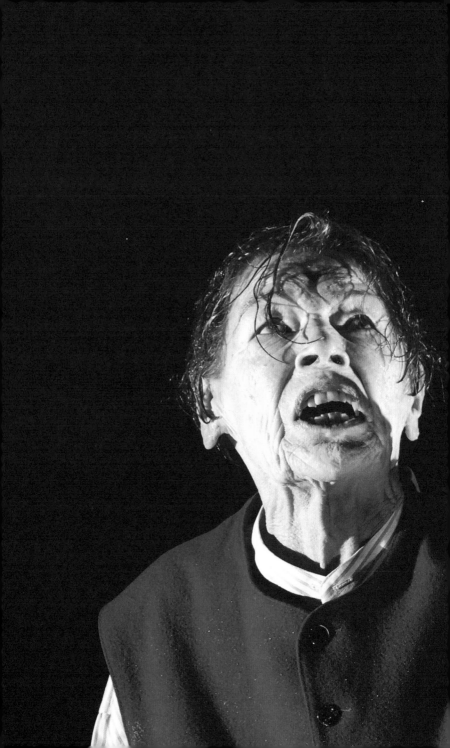

combine the theatrical barnstorming of the old actor-managers with a sly, creepy intimacy. Examined by the undeferential lens, regal authority lets down its guard.

Near the start of Kozintsev's filmed *Hamlet*, there is a lingering close-up of an empty chair. Innokenty Smoktunovksy, who plays the prince, has been sitting in it, quietly disgruntled, during the council meeting at which Claudius discusses Danish foreign policy; he slips away unnoticed, and when Claudius turns towards him there is only that vacant place in the corner. On stage this would hardly register, but the camera directs us to think about it – an image of bereavement, of neurotic distraction, of a power vacuum? Over and above all that, it suggests that the role of Hamlet is a vacancy waiting to be filled, not a seat of state reserved for the elocutionary anointed. Today we have Hamlets of many kinds, confused young men with varying emotional problems. In recent productions, Ben Whishaw was tearful and insecure after a damaged adolescence, David Tennant relieved his pain in bouts of hyperactive playfulness, Jude Law vented an obsessive rage, Benedict Cumberbatch retreated into self-deprecating irony, Andrew Scott twitched nervously, and Rory Kinnear looked baffled and dismayed by the moral morass in which he floundered. None of them bothered to give Hamlet princely airs.

The latest and most valiant of the king actors happens to be a queen – or perhaps not. In 2016, at the age of eighty, after twenty-three years spent as a politician, Glenda Jackson returned to the theatre to play King Lear at the Old Vic. The play's title remained intact, as did the pronouns in the text; Jackson's mettlesome vigour and the scathing eloquence of her jagged, edgy voice, together with her cropped hair and billowing shirt, made Lear's gender irrelevant. The point was not to demand equal opportunity, which may have prompted the casting of Helen Mirren as a maternal Prospera in Taymor's *Tempest* or Tamsin Greig as a lesbian Malvolia in a National Theatre production of *Twelfth*

Night. We are human beings first, only secondarily classified as men, women or something in between, and Jackson – thin, apparently fragile, especially when she tore off her skimpy garments in the storm, but all the same titanic – was moulded from what Keats in his sonnet on *King Lear* calls 'impassioned clay'. 'The wonder is he hath endured so long,' says Kent when Lear at last dies. Longevity is one of the octogenarian monarch's achievements, and Jackson's feat of performing the role every day except Sunday for six weeks during a damp London autumn at the same age as the character surely counted as an existential victory. On behalf of us all, she raged against the weather, social iniquities and the misery of mortality; the experience of watching her laid bare the pain of forfeiting power as we age, and uncomfortably warned that we may never arrive at peace or wisdom. Or should we hope to reach 'the promised end', as Lear does, in the middle of a sentence, unaware of what is happening?

In dozens of small details, quieter than her brazen-toned arias of accusation, Jackson physically acted out the poetry, for instance in her sing-song delivery of Lear's bogus vow to 'unburden'd crawl toward death': she elongated the verb in a quavery drawl, then twiddled her fingers in a jaunty mimicry of geriatric gait – indomitable even when pretending to be exhausted. An audience member's inability to remember and preserve all these moments catches the pathos of live performance, which happens on the border between being and not being, and evaporates like breath or like music. The 'poor player', as Macbeth says, will soon be 'heard no more'.

*

Like actors when they try to forget the lines they have memorized and react spontaneously, people in Shakespeare make themselves up as they go along, and write history on the run. Events we know about because they have been certified by ancient sources happen all over again with dumbfounding unpredictability. 'Hector is dead', Troilus reports. He then has to repeat it – 'He's dead', and finally 'Hector is dead; there is no more to say' – because no one wants to believe the news. The time zone of Shakespeare's plays is a perpetual present.

The pictorial stage stifled this poignant, thrilling transitoriness, and Shakespeare was not freed from its stuffy Victorian inertia until 1925, when a Birmingham production directed by H. K. Ayliff dressed Hamlet in golf pants and let him pensively smoke a cigarette. Even more daringly, Ayliff's *Taming of the Shrew* delivered Petruchio and Katherine to their wedding in a battered car, with photographers brandishing flash bulbs to greet them on arrival. But modernizing Shakespeare involved more than the use of modish accessories: it required an intellectual adjustment, which arrived in 1964 when Jan Kott's critical study *Shakespeare Our Contemporary* allied *King Lear* with the absurdism of Samuel Beckett and found in *Richard III* an anticipation of the totalitarian terror that had only too recently ravaged Europe.

Academics resisted: as a student in Oxford I remember hearing Kott described as a 'Polish savant' – both words were slurs. Directors, however, seized on his insistence that Shakespeare's plays were 'existential facts', alive in our time. Under Kott's influence, Roman Polanski's film of *Macbeth* begins with corpses scattered on a muddy beach, plodding groups of refugees, and a skeletal witch who pushes her cart like Mother Courage foraging through the detritus of history. Kott emphasized the casual cruelty of Shakespeare's plays, which bracingly lacked the lily-livered humanitarianism of the nineteenth century. To prove the point, Polanski made bear-baiting the festive entertainment at Macbeth's court. Instead of a wispy fairy tale, Kott saw *A Midsummer Night's Dream* as a coldly perverse, even bestial orgy. Peter Brook's production in 1970 consequently awarded Bottom a donkey's imposing penis, and turned Cobweb, Mustardseed and Moth into muscular acrobats who performed circus tricks with spinning plates or took to the air on swings and a trapeze. Music was provided by a percussive band supplemented by hacksaw blades, plastic hoses, African noise-makers and an alarm clock. Brook set his *Dream* in a white gymnasium, blank because, as he enigmatically remarked, it represented 'nothingness', lacking fussy Victorian furniture. The critic John Simon deplored the production as an act of 'Bardicide', which was all to the good if it killed off the notion of Shakespeare as a trusted supplier of glum tragic sobriety or hearty comic merriment.

Shakespeare's 'living memory' depends on his being timely, not exempted from time as classics supposedly are. His habit was to jumble historical periods, which effectively cancelled history. It worried Johnson that *A Midsummer Night's Dream* makes Theseus and the Amazons coeval with 'the Gothic mythology of fairies'; Bottom and the artisans belong in a third epoch. *King Lear* presumably happens in prehistoric Britain, which is why James Barry included Stonehenge in his painting of the final scene, yet Lear swears by Apollo, Kent's belief in the sanctity of kingship is medieval, and Edmund's adoption of Nature as his goddess marks him as a Renaissance freethinker. Space is variable, shifting from a palace to a hovel to a cliff that isn't there, and chronological time can also be suspended: the action takes place wherever we are during the three hours we spend watching it.

The theatre has at last caught up with Shakespeare's anachronistic practice. Rupert Goold's production of *Richard III* in the summer of 2016 began in a Leicester car park where a hole had recently been dug to exhume the crookback king's skeleton. Ralph Fiennes's Richard – a mesmeric snake, cold-bloodedly incapable of human feeling – materialized out of the past through this tunnel, and was swallowed by it again at the end. The pit also threatened to disgorge the Tory politicians who were then back-

stabbing each other as they scrambled for power after the referendum on British membership of the European Union. Fiennes remarked in an interview that one of the secessionists, Michael Gove, closely resembled Richard III, with 'his protestations about "I could never lead, it's not in my DNA to lead"'. Goold's initial preference had been to model the character on Gove's former ally Boris Johnson, whom he called 'physically strange and yet sexually predatory... inherently comic, outside the rules, of questionable motives, ultimately ambitious' – lethal despite his buffoonery. Coincidentally, Johnson had signed a lucrative contract to write a biography of Shakespeare, which he shelved to concentrate on ensuring that England would revert to being a sceptred isle. It might have better if he had written the book.

Goold has also set *The Merchant of Venice* in a Las Vegas casino, presenting Portia as the prize bachelorette in a televised game show and Bassanio as a money-grubbing contestant who deceives her about his long-term sexual liaison with Antonio. What looked at first like a glib satire on consumerism and celebrity ended as a double tragedy, with Portia in a state of nervous collapse after discovering the truth about her mercenary new husband while Ian McDiarmid's Shylock, morally crushed and financially ruined, crawled up the aisle of the theatre towards the door, so uncomfortably close to the feet of the audience that he seemed to be ground underfoot. In Goold's Las Vegas, television falsified human relations. Portia and Nerissa began as shiny products of cosmetology, with fake smiles and rehearsed patter, and even Launcelot Gobbo fancied himself as an Elvis impersonator. Enabling us to record and replay ourselves, technology has made performers of us all; now the mirror held up to nature is the screen of an iPhone, on which, striking unnatural poses, we star in the movie of our own on-going lives. Robert Icke, directing *Hamlet* in 2017, explored the politics of this panopticon. Video monitors and a closed-circuit surveillance system spied on a digital world in which shaky pixillated replicas of what once were human beings wandered like ghosts. Hamlet's father was captured on the prowl by security cameras, and Fortinbras existed only in video relays to the country his troops were invading. The paranoia of Hamlet seemed like a rational response to a society in which all surfaces are simulacra and reality is virtual.

Nicholas Hytner's *Timon of Athens* in 2012 made the profligate tycoon a casualty of London's financial industry – cast out of its glazed towers, cold-shouldered in the art galleries where profits are laundered, forced to cobble together his exiled shelter from cardboard boxes in an urban waste. Daniel Kramer, who directed *Romeo and Juliet* at Shakespeare's Globe in the summer of 2017, saw this play too as a critique of 'the grotesquerie of capitalism', with the lovers as 'rich kids who have this expensive world of branded merchandise at their fingertips and would rather press the detonator on it than participate in its rituals'. Two terrorist attacks on nearby bridges across the Thames confirmed Kramer's view of Romeo and Tybalt as exemplars of 'the new violence', which specializes in killing sprees that are viciously random and also self-sanctifying. A *Macbeth* directed by Rufus Norris at the National Theatre in 2018 propelled Shakespeare's warriors into an imminent apocalyptic future of gruesomeness and grunge, in which people are expendable, nature is extinct, and only a wilderness of indestructible plastic litter remains.

Shakespeare's plays sometimes seem to be a nightmare from which the present is trying to awake. The week before the American presidential election in 2016, Ivo van Hove's *Kings of War* – a digest of *Henry V* and *VI* with *Richard III* mixed in – travelled from Amsterdam to Brooklyn. Towards the end of the long performance, the text moved sideways from Dutch to English for a few seconds: after Richard III's abrasive showdown with his sister-in-law, the actor Hans Kesting inserted an aside

overleaf
Gregg Henry as Julius Caesar at the Delacorte Theater.

from Donald Trump's recent debate with Hillary Clinton, snarling 'Such a nasty woman'. The laughter of the audience did not alter the electoral outcome.

The following summer in New York, Oskar Eustis's production of *Julius Caesar* at the Delacorte Theater in Central Park presented Rome's would-be despot as an orange-maned vulgarian who rants on Twitter while cavorting in a gilded bathtub with his Slovenian trophy wife. Three words excerpted from Trump's most unblushing boast about fame and the immunity it confers were added to a speech describing the emperor's loyalists: his fans would not mind, Casca declared, 'if Caesar stabbed their mothers on Fifth Avenue'. Breitbart News decried the staging as an incitement to assassination, and at the performance I attended, right-wing protesters baying abuse interrupted the attack in the Capitol. The actors froze while police and security guards wrestled the invaders to the floor and hauled them away in handcuffs, after which Caesar recovered from his thirty-three gashes and died a second time.

Then, during the rival orations at Caesar's funeral, the man sitting quietly next to me on the aisle sprang up, began to shout, and ran on to the stage. He was an actor, planted there – not a protester, but all the same a citizen and therefore a participant, like everyone else in that open-air room. At this point *Julius Caesar* urges us all to join in by taking sides, though it goes on to demonstrate that both parties are right or perhaps wrong, and leaves us to continue the debate as we re-examine the play on our way home.

'Doubtful it stood,' says the bloodied soldier as he begins his account of the clash between Macbeth and Macdonwald. That is how things usually stand in Shakespeare: the great gift his plays make to us is a radical doubt about who we are, what we might be capable of, and what will happen to us next. Casca, invited to supper by Cassius, agrees to turn up tomorrow 'if I be alive and your mind hold and your dinner worth the eating' – a conditional triplet that casually notices how tenuous our existence is, always at the mercy of the unforeseeable shocks that flesh is heir to and that punctuate the moment-to-moment business of the theatre. 'To be, or not to be' is the unspoken subtext of every scene in every Shakespearean play; Hamlet says it out loud, but leaves his own dubiety unresolved. Frustratingly but fortunately, our business with Shakespeare is always unfinished.

*

Soon after dawn on the day I saw *Julius Caesar*, I joined the queue in the otherwise deserted park to wait for tickets to the free, epidemically popular show. Hours later, before the distribution began at noon, the line straggled into the green, hazy distance. It began to rain; a dog-walker wanted to know why two thousand of us were huddled under the dripping trees. 'You do this for some old British guy?' he asked when it was explained to him. 'Go figure', he said as his pedigree pack dragged him off. Yes, Shakespeare had roused us from our beds, and none of us regretted the wake-up call or the long, weary vigil. We were keen to see our motley selves, our moral confusions and our disagreements or hatreds reflected in what Maecenas in *Antony and Cleopatra* calls 'a spacious mirror'. The conspirators in *Julius Caesar* expected us to be there. After the assassination they pause to reflect that their little drama will be repeated in the future, 'acted over / In states unborn', where Caesar, as Brutus predicts, will 'bleed in sport', as he certainly did that night in Central Park. But our satirical glee was followed by a more sober self-scrutiny as we watched the ensuing havoc: replaying history does not spare us from having to repeat it.

When Prospero abandons the theatre to resume his life or to think about death, he equates the applause of an audience with the remission of sins:

As you from crimes would pardoned be
Let your indulgence set me free.

His last words, less self-evident than the rhyming couplet makes them sound, are either shifty and guilt-wracked or slyly manipulative. Could it be a crime to stage a play, as Prospero has done, or even to see one, which may be why he thinks we are culpable? Actors murder in jest, and we egg them on; in clapping our hands, we absolve them of blame. We also exonerate ourselves by deciding, as Puck recommends, that the offences were committed by shadows, or dismissing it all as an insubstantial pageant. Yet despite this irresponsibility, attendance at the theatre is a communal rite, and as we study behaviour, speculate about motives and assess consequences, a play rehearses a moral reckoning. We constitute a jury, though there is no judge to deliver a final verdict.

Shakespeare, however, questions the theatre's efficacy as a tribunal. While Escalus in *Measure for Measure* deliberates over the case against a bawd and her helpers, Angelo storms out, hoping he will find 'good cause to whip them all'. In *Much Ado About Nothing* the dim-witted constable Dogberry captures a villain, but only by accident. And what of the Venetian court that expropriates Shylock's goods? The stage is a zone of confrontation and conflict on to which all the instabilities of our actual world overflow. Problems have to be tackled repeatedly, seen from different angles, like Shakespearean productions that catch our conscience, as Hamlet puts it, by showing us something new.

The plays are about characters in action, and about our internalized actions as we follow them. Emotions are movements too, and as we watch and listen we are liable to feel our minds changing, our values challenged. Inside the wooden O – a circle that contains infinity and yet symbolizes zero – our avatars successively crawl, skip, sprint, stride, trudge, shuffle and totter through the ages of man, compressing lifetimes into an afternoon or evening. As well as travelling ahead in time, these surrogates gyrate in space, and their whirligig reversals show how hectically we are spun round on the globe while we struggle to keep our balance. Our end may be scripted, foreordained, as if by the letter in which Hamlet requests the execution of those who bear it as soon as they step ashore; still, given the frequency of shipwrecks or attacks by pirates or other misadventures, we can never be sure when or how we will reach what the self-doomed Othello bluntly calls 'my butt'.

Shakespeare combines tragedy and comedy, as we all do in our biological entrances and exits. We cry when we are born; with luck we might possibly die smiling, glad to have got through an existence as precarious as the brief flickering of a candle. In between, we should heed the advice of Shakespeare's noblest Roman, who on the night before his final battle refuses to dwell on his own impending fate or on the recent death of his wife. As if preparing to start a performance rather than end one, he briskly says 'Well, to our work alive.' That is our cue. Shakespeare wrote the plays, and the rest of us – alone and together, offstage or on it – act them out.

Chronology

The dates of first performances of Shakespeare's plays are difficult or impossible to determine. The list below follows the order of composition proposed by recent editors, who often rely on circumstantial guesswork.

1589–91 *The Two Gentlemen of Verona*

1590–1 *The Taming of the Shrew*

1591–2 *Henry VI Parts 1–3*

1592–3 *Richard III*

1593–4 *Titus Andronicus*

1593–4 *The Comedy of Errors, Love's Labour's Lost*

1594–5 *A Midsummer Night's Dream, Romeo and Juliet*

1595 *Richard II*

1595–6 *King John*

1596–7 *The Merchant of Venice*

1597–8 *Henry IV Parts 1 and 2, The Merry Wives of Windsor*

1598–9 *Much Ado About Nothing*

1599 *Henry V, Julius Caesar*

1599–1601 *Hamlet*

1600 *As You Like It*

1601 *Twelfth Night*

1602 *Troilus and Cressida*

1603–4 *Measure for Measure, Othello*

1604–5 *All's Well That Ends Well*

1605–6 *Timon of Athens, King Lear*

1606 *Macbeth, Antony and Cleopatra*

1607–8 *Pericles*, perhaps in collaboration with George Wilkins

1608 *Coriolanus*

1609–10 *The Winter's Tale*

1610 *Cymbeline*

1610–11 *The Tempest*

1612–13 *Henry VIII*, with John Fletcher

1613–14 *The Two Noble Kinsmen*, with John Fletcher

Further reading

Biography and textual history

Stephen Greenblatt, *Will in the World: How Shakespeare Became Shakespeare*

S. Schoenbaum, *William Shakespeare: A Compact Documentary Life*

  Shakespeare's Lives

James Shapiro, *1599: A Year in the Life of Shakespeare*

  1608: Shakespeare and the Year of Lear

  Contested Will: Who Wrote Shakespeare?

Paul Edmondson (ed), *Shakespeare Beyond Doubt: Evidence, Argument, Controversy*

David Bevington, *Shakespeare and Biography*

Emma Smith, *Shakespeare's First Folio: Four Centuries of an Iconic Book*

Reputation and reception

Michael Dobson, *The Making of the National Poet*

Christian Deelman, *The Great Shakespeare Jubilee*

Jonathan Bate, *Shakespeare and the English Romantic Imagination*

F. E. Halliday, *The Cult of Shakespeare*

Marjorie Garber, *Shakespeare After All*

Gordon McMullan and Zoe Wilcox (ed.), *Shakespeare in Ten Acts*

Stephen Orgel, *Imagining Shakespeare: A History of Texts and Visions*

James Shapiro (ed.), *Shakespeare in America: An Anthology from the Revolution to Now*

Gary Taylor, *Reinventing Shakespeare*

Criticism and adaptation

W. K. Wimsatt (ed.), *Dr Johnson on Shakespeare*

R. A. Foakes, R. A. (ed.), *Coleridge on Shakespeare*

William Hazlitt, *Characters of Shakespeare's Plays*

Jonathan Bate (ed.), *The Romantics on Shakespeare*

Oswald LeWinter (ed.), *Shakespeare in Europe*

Edwin Wilson (ed.), *Shaw on Shakespeare*

Dorothy Collins (ed.), *G. K. Chesterton on Shakespeare*

W. H. Auden, *Lectures on Shakespeare* (edited by Arthur C. Kirsch)

   The Dyer's Hand and Other Essays

Giovanni Cianci and Caroline Patey (ed.), *Will the Modernist: Shakespeare and the European Historical Avant-Gardes*

Northrop Frye, *Northrop Frye on Shakespeare*

Jan Kott, *Shakespeare Our Contemporary*

John Gross (ed.), *After Shakespeare: An Anthology*

Michael Dobson and Stanley Wells (ed.), *The Oxford Companion to Shakespeare*

Jonathan Dollimore and Alan Sinfield (ed.), *Political Shakespeare: Essays in Cultural Materialism*

Frank Kermode, *Shakespeare's Language*

R. W. Maslen, *Shakespeare and Comedy*

Russ McDonald (ed.), *Shakespeare: An Anthology of Criticism and Theory 1945-2000*

James Shapiro (ed.), *Shakespeare in America: An Anthology from the Revolution to Now*

Robert Shaughnessy (ed.), *The Cambridge Companion to Shakespeare and Popular Culture*

Shakespeare and the other arts

Daniel Albright, *Musicking Shakespeare*

Gary Schmidgall, *Shakespeare and Opera*

Phyllis Hartnoll (ed.), *Shakespeare in Music*

W. Moelwyn Merchant, *Shakespeare and the Artist*

Jane Martineau et al., *Shakespeare in Art*, Dulwich Picture Gallery catalogue, 2003

Geoffrey Ashton (ed.), *Shakespeare and British Art,* Yale Center for British Art catalogue, New Haven, 1981

John Christian (ed.), *Shakespeare and Western Art*, Isetan Museum of Art catalogue, Tokyo, 1992

Mirko Ilic and Steven Heller (ed.), *Presenting Shakespeare: 1,1000 Posters from Around the World*

Shakespeare in performance

Stanley Wells (ed.), *Shakespeare in the Theatre: An Anthology of Criticism*

Robert Speaight, *Shakespeare on the Stage*

Richard Findlater, *The Player Kings*

John Gielgud, *Shakespeare: Hit or Miss?*

Brook, Peter, *The Quality of Mercy: Reflections on Shakespeare*

Dominic Dromgoole, *Will & Me*

Hamlet: Globe to Globe

Abigail Rokison-Woodall, *Shakespeare in the Theatre: Nicholas Hytner*

Antony Sher, *Year of the King*

Year of the Mad King: The Lear Diaries

Year of the Fat Knight: The Falstaff Diaries

Michael Anderegg, *Orson Welles, Shakespeare, and Popular Culture*

Grigori Kozintsev, *King Lear: The Space of Tragedy*

Shakespeare: Time and Conscience

Roger Manvell, *Shakespeare and the Film*

Daniel Rosenthal, *Shakespeare on Screen*

Mark Thornton Burnett and Ramona Wray (ed.), *Shakespeare, Film, Fin de Siècle*

Acknowledgments

The idea of writing this book arose as the chance result of a conversation with Rupert Christiansen. My thanks to him for being its unwitting 'onlie begetter', to Caroline Dawnay for urging me to go ahead, and in pride of place to my editor Richard Milbank, who managed to be both exacting and accommodating, and made me anxious to please him. Later stages of production were expertly overseen by Georgina Blackwell.

Over the years, my experience of Shakespeare has been happily collaborative. Rereading the plays revived memories of conversations and lively arguments about them with the students I taught in Oxford between 1973 and 2011. Further back, it was my rare good fortune to spend Saturday mornings in the summer of 1969 at Shakespeare tutorials with the fabled Hugo Dyson – a wise jester, and a warmly encouraging elder.

Later in 1969 I made my first trip to Stratford, to see Judi Dench and Donald Sinden in *Twelfth Night*. I am grateful to Jorge Calado for his company on that occasion, for the gramophone record of a favourite Shakespeare sonnet he made from memory in a booth at Paddington Station, for a book about Olivier's Othello - and for so much else in the years since then.

Index

Illustrations are in *italics*.

H